MARRIAGE DONE RIGHT

Marriage Done Right

ONE MAN, ONE WOMAN

Jim Daly
PRESIDENT, FOCUS ON THE FAMILY
WITH PAUL BATURA

REGNERY
FAITH

Author is represented by Ambassador Literary, Nashville, TN

Cataloging-in-Publication data on file with the Library of Congress

ISBN 978-1-62157-519-1

Published in the United States by
Regnery Faith
An imprint of Regnery Publishing
A Division of Salem Media Group
300 New Jersey Ave NW
Washington, DC 20001
www.RegneryFaith.com

Manufactured in the United States of America

10 9 8 7 6 5 4 3 2 1

Books are available in quantity for promotional or premium use. For information on discounts and terms, please visit our website: www.Regnery.com.

Distributed to the trade by
Perseus Distribution
250 West 57th Street
New York, NY 10107

To all Christ followers who want to make a difference not only in their own marriages but in the lives and marriages of others.

Contents

Part III: The Twelve Traits of Highly Successful Marriages

A marriage itself is something which has to be created, so that together we become a new creature. To marry is the biggest risk in human relations that a person can take.... If we commit ourselves to one person for life this is not, as many people think, a rejection of freedom; rather it demands the courage to move into all the risks of freedom, and the risk of love which is permanent; into that love which is not possession, but participation.... It takes a lifetime to learn another person.... When love is not possession, but participation, then it is part of that co-creation which is our human calling, and which implies such risk that it is often rejected.

—Madeleine L'Engle, *The Irrational Season*

Being in love is a good thing, but it is not the best thing. There are many things below it, but there are also things above it. You cannot make it the basis of a whole life. It is a noble feeling, but it is still a feeling. Now no feeling can be relied on to last in its full intensity, or even to last at all. Knowledge can last, principles can last, habits can last; but feelings come and go. And in fact, whatever people say, the state called "being in love" usually does not last. If the old fairy-tale ending "They lived happily ever after" is taken to mean "They felt for the next fifty years exactly as they felt the day before they were married," then it says what probably never was nor ever would be true, and would be highly undesirable if it were. Who could bear to live in that excitement for even five years? What would become of your work, your appetite, your sleep, your friendships? But, of course, ceasing to be "in love" need not mean ceasing to love. Love in this second sense—love as distinct from "being in love"—is not merely a feeling. It is a deep unity, maintained by the will and deliberately strengthened by habit; reinforced by (in Christian marriages) the grace which both partners ask, and receive, from God. They can have this love for each other even at those moments when they do not like each other; as you love yourself even when you do not like yourself. They can retain this love even when each would easily, if they allowed themselves, be "in love" with someone else. "Being in love" first moved them to promise fidelity: this quieter love enables them to keep the promise. It is on this love that the engine of marriage is run: being in love was the explosion that started it.

—C. S. Lewis, *Mere Christianity*

Marriage is an adventure, like going to war.

—G. K. Chesterton

Let marriage be held in honor among all....

—Hebrews 13:4, ESV

PROLOGUE

Why Should We Care about Marriage?

The scene on the sidewalk outside the U.S. Supreme Court was chaotic. It was the morning of Tuesday, April 28, 2015, and I was in town for the historic oral arguments of *Obergefell v. Hodges*, the soon-to-be-landmark case that would ultimately guarantee same-sex couples the right to marry. Spring had sprung in Washington, D.C. The sky was blue and the air was brisk but comfortable. As I walked toward the sun-drenched marble plaza surrounding the courthouse, the smell of freshly cut grass filled the air and flowering trees framed my view.

The idyllic moment, however, quickly dissolved in a cacophony of shouts, chants, and speeches, each voice competing with the others for attention. Bullhorns and loudspeakers amplified the noise. Nearly every inch of the wide sidewalk along First Street was occupied by individuals and special-interest groups. American and rainbow flags fluttered in the breeze. Banners and signs from both sides bobbed up and down in the air. Some were brazen. Others were more muted. It was American democracy on display. The dialogue was civil, for the most part, but decidedly spirited and robust.

It was obvious that those supporting the traditional one-man, one-woman definition of marriage were substantially outnumbered, but I was impressed to see so many young people standing strong for God's design for marriage. I recognized many of our friends and allies in the crowds. But make no mistake—emotions and tensions were running high.

I weaved through the raucous throng and up off the sidewalk. A policeman waved me past the metal barriers separating the protestors from the plaza. Just to the left of the familiar steps, columns, and large bronze doors, I made my way to the court's side entrance. It was just after nine in the morning. As I slipped inside, the din of the activists quickly faded. I glanced back over my shoulder and then turned to greet a security guard. It was almost time for the highly anticipated two-and-a-half-hour hearing.

Two months later and two thousand miles away, I watched the announcement of the disappointing five-to-four decision from my desk in Colorado Springs. It was Friday, June 26, 2015. Truth be told, I wasn't shocked. Since that morning inside the courtroom, I couldn't shake the sense that at least four and probably five of the justices were eager to redefine marriage. As I listened to both sides argue their case that day, I kept thinking it would be a travesty for the justices to ignore the views of the fifty-one million Americans who had voted in the past decade to preserve the traditional definition of marriage as a union of one man and one woman.[1] Of course, marriage is already defined by the natural law. But understanding that not everyone acknowledges that authority and that the Constitution is silent on the subject of marriage, I've long believed that it's up to the people to decide how marriage should be defined. After all, less than twenty years ago only but a handful of people thought it even needed to be defined. It was self-evident.

Yet from the line of questioning coming from the bench, it was apparent that a majority of the justices disagreed with this interpretation of the Constitution.

While Justice Anthony Kennedy initially expressed reluctance to sweep away the immemorial and universal understanding of marriage, he repeatedly asserted that the primary purpose of marriage is to confer dignity on the spouses. Writing for the majority, Kennedy confirmed that line of reasoning, calling the right to marry "central to individual dignity and autonomy" and insisting that same-sex-attracted persons are merely seeking "equal dignity in the eyes of the law."[2]

Several months later, when news of the death of Justice Antonin Scalia reached me, I recalled how energized and engaged he had been during those historic oral arguments. He had warned that the religious liberties of ministers would be in jeopardy if same-sex marriage were declared a constitutional right. "The minister is, to the extent he's conducting a civil marriage, he's an instrument of the States," Scalia reasoned. "I don't see how you could possibly allow that minister to say, I will only marry a man and a woman. I will not marry two men." Leaving it to the states to legislate same-sex marriage, he argued, allows them to protect the rights of dissenters. "[Y]ou can make an exception. The State can say, 'Yes, two men can marry,' but ministers who do not believe in same-sex marriage will still be authorized to conduct marriages on behalf of the State. You can't do that once it is a constitutional proscription."[3]

We will know in time if the great justice was prescient. I believe his concerns were well founded. As he wrote in his blistering dissent, "This is a naked judicial claim to legislative power, a claim fundamentally at odds with our system of government. A system of government that makes people subordinate to a committee of nine unelected lawyers does not deserve to be called a democracy."[4]

Justice Kennedy seems to have a novel understanding of the word "dignity." Whereas Christians and natural law theorists have always seen dignity as an inherent attribute of humanity, Kennedy treats it as synonymous with individual autonomy and the right to define oneself. With all due respect, I think he's wrong. Marriage has always been recognized as the institution that binds a man and a woman as husband and wife, to be father and mother to any children their union produces, not as a dignity-conferring domestic arrangement. Alas, Justice Kennedy has a vote—and I do not.

HOW DID WE GET HERE?

The journey toward the redefinition of marriage started decades ago. Today's legal redefinition has its roots in steady and significant cultural change.

The understanding of marriage as the lifelong union of a man and a woman prevailed across cultures for millennia. It protected the children born from that union. Indeed, bringing children into this world has historically been seen as the primary purpose of marriage. Marriage, sex, and childbearing were linked in people's minds and usually in practice.

And then came the sexual revolution, breaking the "iron triangle" of marriage, sex, and childbearing and ushering in monumental changes in our collective worldview and culture.[5]

A pivotal moment came on May 9, 1960, when the Food and Drug Administration approved the sale and use of the pill. As my friend Dr. Al Mohler has observed, this form of birth control turned pregnancy—and thus children—into a choice rather than the natural gift of the marital union. Many contend, moreover, that the marital union itself was weakened by the pill, which facilitated adultery and other forms of nonmarital sex. In some hands, the pill became a human pesticide.

With easy access to birth control and, after the Supreme Court's *Roe v. Wade* decision in 1973, to abortion, it was easier for couples to opt out of marriage. Many did, and cohabitation rates increased thirty-five-fold from 1960 to 2010, further weakening marriage.[6] The devaluing of marriage in favor of merely living together has accelerated even more among the millennial generation.

No-fault divorce arrived in California in 1969[7]—with Governor Ronald Reagan's approval—and had spread to every other state by 1985.[8]

Taken together, these developments helped reduce marriage, in the eyes of many, to a solemnized expression of emotional love. No longer did the majority of people hold a conjugal view of marriage as the lifelong, exclusive union of a man and woman who, in most cases, have and raise their children together.

SHOULDN'T TWO PEOPLE BE ALLOWED TO LOVE EACH OTHER?

Once that conjugal understanding of marriage was undermined, it became easier for people to accept a definition of marriage as the union of *any* two persons, regardless of their sex—a definition based on the philosophical shrug of the shoulders, "Love is love."

The Church, unfortunately, made up of fallible and imperfect people, didn't do all it could to respond to this rapid cultural change. When we could have offered a vision of God's plan for marriage and the family, many of us were ourselves caught up in the sexual revolution.

We could have encouraged young couples in love to marry, but we told them to postpone marriage until they had a college education, a stable job, and a healthy bank account. No longer was marriage an institution that helped shape and mature young people. Rather, it became the "cherry on top" after they had achieved a certain level of success. We could have offered a bright, shining example of the vitality and joy that can be found in a Christ-centered marriage, but Christian divorce rates rivaled everyone else's.

A HAUNTING QUESTION

No wonder a homosexual activist once asked me, "Since Christians haven't done so well in the arena of marriage, why not let us try?" That sounds like a reasonable question, but what my friend doesn't understand is that God's plan for marriage isn't any less true or wise just because Christians haven't lived it as well as they could have. Despite our shortcomings, God's design—one man and one woman, committed for life, welcoming and raising children together—remains the best model of family there is.

NOTHING ELSE BENEFITS MEN, WOMEN, AND CHILDREN MORE THAN BIBLICAL MARRIAGE

Perhaps even more important, nothing else more beautifully represents the Gospel. And so this is why it's critically important that we care about marriage.

They say that law is downstream from culture. If that's true, then the judicial imposition of same-sex marriage—first in Massachusetts in 2004[9] and throughout the country eleven years later—shouldn't have come as a surprise. Furthermore, as Christians, it's important for us to humbly and candidly acknowledge that we bear some of the blame for the downward trajectory of the marriage culture.

OWNING OUR PART OF THE PROBLEM

When my homosexual activist friend challenged me about the mess heterosexuals have made of marriage, I had to acknowledge his point. It's time for us to own up to our own sin and get our own house in order. Though we can educate, encourage, and pray for the culture, we cannot control it. But we do have it within us to take our own marital commitment seriously. The most powerful way we can do that is by loving our spouse the way Christ loves His Church.

After decades of no-fault divorce, many Christians simply tire of their spouses and allow themselves to be whisked away by a fantasy, that the grass will be greener on the other side of the fence. Premarital sex and cohabitation have become commonplace among those professing to be Christian. Here at Focus on the Family, calls to our counseling department reveal that Internet pornography is destroying marriages on a daily basis. And many persons, particularly younger evangelicals, are simply choosing to bypass the altar altogether. In fact, I saw a recent report saying that for the first time ever, more than half of American adults are unmarried.

As we Christians struggle to uphold one-man, one-woman marriage, the trends are not in our favor. Does that mean that we should shrink back and admit that marriage is a lost cause? On the contrary, I think our witness to the beauty and goodness of true marriage becomes all the more important. It will be up to us to show a fraying culture that marriage is so much more than "just a piece of paper" or an association of any two or more persons who profess to love each other. It is a sacred union of a man and a woman that confers myriad benefits on the spouses, their children, and society at large—benefits that cannot be replicated by any other relationship. I would go so far as to say a society cannot flourish, or even long survive, without stable marriages at its core.

For all its material benefits, the marital bond, for Christians, is above all the mysterious symbol, a miniature representation, of the relationship Jesus has with His bride, the Church (Eph. 5:31–32). When we demonstrate unwavering commitment and sacrificial love to our spouses, we are mirroring to our culture the very love Christ has for His people. What an awesome responsibility and privilege!

That's why I urge Christians to pour themselves into their marriages. Research tells us that the divorce rate for Christians who take their faith seriously is notably lower than that of the general population, but even so it is still far too high. What a testimony to our neighbors it would be if the divorce rate of believers were but a fraction of the general population's.

THE ROAD AHEAD

Reporters regularly ask me when I'm finally going to "pivot" on the subject of marriage. In other words, what's it going to take to persuade me that Christians need to "evolve with the times" and "go with the flow" regarding the new definition of marriage? Others have challenged, even taunted, me about being on the "wrong side of history." For a point of comparison, they often cite Christians who, back in the day, wrongly opposed interracial marriage or supported slavery. There is much to discuss on the subject, but I would point out that racism kept the races apart. That's obviously a detrimental thing. Marriage, however, unites the two sexes, and that's a good thing. Marriage must be color-blind, but it cannot be sex-blind. Men and women—regardless of their race—can unite in marriage. Children—regardless of their race—need moms and dads. As for those worried about ending up on the wrong side of history, I remind them that history is long. In the end, I want to be on God's side of history. Nothing else matters to me.

This book isn't a screed against the legalization of same-sex marriage. Nor is it a rallying cry for traditionalists to wage war with the culture in the hope of returning to a time that never really existed. Instead, it's a candid and passionate attempt to challenge each one of us to look within his own heart and examine his own life and behavior. Marriage is not an entitlement. It's a gift that too many of us have squandered. Rather than pointing our fingers at others, I want us to look in the mirror.

When federal agents are trained to detect counterfeit currency, they don't study bogus bills; they study the real thing. They pay close attention to the look and feel of the genuine currency. Likewise, if we want to preserve and promote God's definition of marriage, it's a good idea to spend our time examining His plan and His purpose for it, not just for the culture, but for our own lives as well.

PART I

The Institution

CHAPTER ONE

Miracle, Mystery, and Wonder

When [the convert] has entered the Church, he finds that the Church is much larger inside than it is outside.[1]

—G. K. Chesterton

On a Wednesday evening in the summer of 1985, I decided on a whim to do something I had never before done. After a long day of sales calls with my employer, I found my way to a service at Lake Arrowhead Christian Fellowship, a church in the beautiful mountains of the San Bernardino National Forest. I did not attend regularly and knew very few people there, but in the middle of his sermon on salvation, the pastor—whom I did not know—stopped abruptly and walked directly toward me. "I have a word from the Lord for you," he said, looking down at me. "The Lord has picked out a wife for you. She will have a heart for the things of God." He paused and then continued. "And in the years to come, you will spread the gospel of Jesus Christ to people all around the world. She'll be your crown."

To say that I was stunned by such a declaration would be an understatement. I had decided to take a break from dating. It was just something the Lord had laid on my heart. As a result of that decision, my head was clearing and my prayer life was improving. It felt great to devote my full attention to my spiritual development, not the pursuit of a pretty girl. But I was receptive to what this man said to me. I didn't write him off as a crank. At the same time, I was perplexed and a little uncomfortable, and I left the service that evening thinking I would never return to that particular church.

Three days later, I had the privilege of serving as the best man in my friend Dan's wedding. Even though it was their big day, Dan and his bride, Tina, worked like crazy to get me together with Tina's friend Jean Stephens. At their insistence, Jean and I danced once and made some small talk. When I returned to my table, I couldn't believe what I heard myself say to my friend Victor: "I think I met the woman I'm going to marry."

But life got busy, and it was nine months before I saw Jean again. Once again our friends tried to play Cupid, arranging for me to take her to an outdoor Amy Grant concert in Newport Beach. As we enjoyed our picnic dinner in the twilight of that warm evening, I think we both realized something good was happening, but we kept our thoughts to ourselves.

Jean had to return to the University of California at Davis, where she was a pre-veterinary student, in September. Utterly love-struck, I quit my job and moved in with my brother Mike, who happened to live about forty miles from Jean's school. For two semesters I burned through savings and the income from a few odd jobs while Jean finished her degree.

Our dating life was lots of fun. We talked and talked and talked. In the spring I bought a ring and proposed (with her father's permission) under the shade of a large Santa Barbara oak tree. Thankfully, she said yes. There's more to the story, but I'll save it for later. For now, I'll just say that when I think back on those days, I'm reminded that though man has his plans, God will always have His way (Prov. 19:21).

GOD IS THE MASTER CHESS PLAYER

It's fascinating to look back at the many mysterious twists and turns in our lives, especially in the path that leads to marriage. How do two people, often with widely disparate backgrounds, happen to meet at just the right time for both of them? When it comes to the sovereignty of God, I don't believe in coincidence. The psalmist writes, "His kingdom rules over all" (103:19, ESV) and "He does all that he pleases" (115:3, ESV). Indeed He does. If I were to make a chart of all the events and relationships that led me to Jean, I would need a sheet of paper the size of a basketball court. To meet Jean, I had to be friends with Dan, who had to be friends with Tina. I met Dan because we were exchange students together—in Japan. I went to Japan because... well, you get the picture. If you're married, I suspect you have a similar story. As C. S. Lewis famously observed, "For a Christian, there are, strictly speaking, no chances. A secret Master of the Ceremonies has been at work."[2]

But the true "mystery" of marriage is not in the meeting of the two people who become husband and wife but in the Maker of the institution itself. In God's economy, marriage was the final piece to the creation puzzle. Why else would Adam have exclaimed, "At last!" when he first saw Eve (Gen. 2:23, NLT)? He was lonely. "But for Adam there was not found a helper comparable to him," we read in Genesis (Gen. 2:20, NKJV). In other words, things just weren't right until Eve arrived: "The Lord God said, 'It is not good that man should be alone; I will make him a helper comparable to him'" (Gen. 2:18, NKJV).

God created a separate person in Eve, but He did it with a rib from Adam. "This is now bone of my bones and flesh of my flesh," Adam rejoices; "she shall be called Woman, because she was taken out of Man" (Gen. 2:23, NKJV). Forevermore, Adam is part of Eve, and Eve is part of Adam. This is one of many reasons why we're to take our marital vows so seriously. We're to see marriage not merely as a contract but as a covenant. It's not an agreement with loopholes or termination clauses. When you pledge yourself to your spouse, you're entering into the most intimate of all relationships. As we read in Genesis, when a couple are united in marriage "they shall become one flesh" (Gen 2:24, NKJV).

OBLIGATION AND OPPORTUNITY

Dr. Albert Mohler reflects on the profound and mysterious nature of the marriage relationship: "According to the Bible, marriage is not primarily about self-esteem and personal fulfillment, nor is it just one lifestyle option among others. The Bible is clear in presenting a picture of marriage that is rooted in the glory of God made evident in creation itself. The man and the woman are made for each other, and the institution of marriage is given to humanity as both opportunity and obligation."[3]

I think most of us would acknowledge that marriage is an obligation, but how many of us also see it as an opportunity? An opportunity for what? To have guilt-free sex? To have someone by your side, to help you through the ups and downs of life? To conceive and raise children together? To provide for and to be provided for? Perhaps all of the above, but Dr. Mohler is referring to something beyond practical needs or pleasure. And therein lies the challenge. If we're honest, most of us have to admit that we think about what we get out of marriage more often than we think about what we give. We're inherently selfish people who keep score with our spouses. But true intimacy doesn't come from taking from your partner; it comes from giving.

I learned this lesson the hard way during the first few years of our marriage. We started with a bang—lots of travel, the thrill of being newlyweds, and dreams of a lifetime together. But sometime during our second year of marriage, the dark clouds moved in. One night when I got into bed, Jean was sobbing. "What's wrong?" I asked. Wiping away the tears, she said, "I just don't think you should stay married to me." My heart sank. What on earth was going on?

When I pressed her, it became clear that Jean was wrestling with depression and a lack of confidence that she'd be a good mother once we started having children. I worried about whether I'd be a good dad myself, especially since I didn't have a solid example to follow. Although I loved my father, he was unreliable. As I shared in my autobiography, *Finding Home*,[4] he was a chronic gambler, an alcoholic who once threatened my mom with a hammer, and at one point suicidal. He divorced my mother when I was just a child. I didn't learn the first thing about how to love, cherish, or provide for a wife from him.

Prior to this heart-rending moment, my initial reaction to my wife's ongoing insecurities was to give her pep talks. The way out of trouble, it seemed to me then, was always to face a problem head-on with positive thinking. One night, after an especially difficult conversation and another of my spirited pleas for mental toughness, Jean said to me through tears, "You know, Jim, not everyone can pull himself up by his bootstraps."

Lying next to my dear wife that night in bed, I finally began to get it. "Jean, you're right," I said. "I'm sorry. I will commit to trying to see things from other people's point of view. It seems to me that there are only two options for us, because divorce is not an option.

We can do marriage one of two ways: happily or unhappily." I added, "With all of the stuff that's gone on in my life, I'd much rather do this happily. I am here to listen, and most of all I'm here to help."

Building on that bedrock of commitment, we began Christian counseling. With help, we were able to untangle the difficulties in our background that were keeping us from growing closer. To this day, I occasionally struggle to show compassion and empathy, which come naturally to Jean. She'll cry with a neighbor when his dog dies. Growing up in a dysfunctional home, I developed a "survivalist" mentality, gritting my teeth and grinning my way through life, certain that a resilient spirit would win the day. That approach might work if you're stranded on a desert island, but it can make for a difficult approach if you're married to a kindhearted woman like Jean.

I continue to learn that one of the best ways I can serve my wife is to listen to her thoughts, insecurities, and fears without passing judgment or serving up a quick solution. Of course I can offer perspective and input when and where appropriate, but what she craves is my ear, and she deeply desires to be understood. I have also learned that she wants *me* to be vulnerable with *her*. Through the counseling, I discovered that my "survivalist" instinct—"If it's going to be, it's up to me!"—doesn't encourage intimacy in marriage. Over time, I've learned to bring down my defenses and share my innermost thoughts with Jean.

MARRIAGE IS A PROFOUND MYSTERY

We can learn a lot about life by studying the lives of others, and I especially love reading about U.S. presidents. In recent years, a misleading narrative of Abraham and Mary Todd Lincoln's marriage has emerged, with some scholars suggesting that isolation, depression, and even mental illness left it nearly dysfunctional.

It's true that this marriage of sharply contrasting personalities—he was mild mannered, she high strung—faced its share of difficulties. A friend once challenged Abe for giving in too easily to his wife, calling him a pushover. The president responded, "If you knew how little harm it does me and how much good it does her, you wouldn't wonder that I am meek."[5] But in November 1842, just a week after having slipped a ring on Mary's finger that was engraved with the phrase "Love is Eternal," the young groom wrote to a friend, "Nothing new here, except my marrying, which to me, is a matter of profound wonder."[6]

The Apostle Paul gets to the very heart of that wonder and the purpose of marriage in his letter to the Ephesians:

> Wives, submit to your own husbands, as to the Lord. For the husband is the head of the wife even as Christ is the head of the church, his body, and is himself its Savior. Now as the church submits to Christ, so also wives should submit in everything to their husbands.
>
> Husbands, love your wives, as Christ loved the church and gave himself up for her, that he might sanctify her, having cleansed her by the washing of water with the word, so that he might present the church to himself in splendor, without spot or wrinkle or any such thing, that she might be holy and without blemish. In the same way husbands should love their wives as their own bodies. He who loves his wife loves himself. For no one ever hated his own flesh, but nourishes and cherishes it, just as Christ does the church, because we are members of his body. "Therefore a man shall leave his father and mother and hold fast to his wife, and the two shall become one flesh." This mystery is profound, and I am saying that it refers to

> Christ and the church. However, let each one of you love his wife as himself, and let the wife see that she respects her husband. (Eph. 5:22–33, ESV)

This is a loaded passage with profound implications, and it makes many of us cringe. The term "submission," we fear, sounds hopelessly backward. I recently saw a panel of women on television heatedly discussing the actress Candace Cameron Bure's statement in a book and in interviews that she had decided to live out biblical submission in her twenty-year marriage to the professional hockey player Valeri Bure. Bure defined biblical submission as "meekness, not weakness" and "strength under control; bridled strength."[7] But the women I heard on TV weren't buying it. In their view, "submission" means blindly following your husband's every capricious whim in humiliating subservience. Indeed, the biblical concept of submission is easily lost in modern-day translation. To many outside the Christian faith, the Scriptural principles of marriage that Mrs. Bure was citing are at best outdated and at worst foolish.

Missing from this discussion was a very important part of the story: What does the Bible say about the *husband's* role in a marriage? The critics seem to take it for granted that the Bible gives husbands a free pass to be tyrants. But nothing could be further from the truth.

There are at least three points about a husband's role that critics should consider before dismissing what the Bible has to say about marriage. First, *God calls husbands to love and to continual sacrifice for their wives.* The Apostle Paul compares the love a husband should have for his wife to Christ's love for the Church. For the husband, that means a daily dying to self just as Jesus died for the Church. It's a life of service to his wife, of tending to her needs, and of putting her above all others.

Second, *husbands must submit to God.* Jesus made it clear during His time on earth that He submitted to God the Father (see John 5:19,

6:38, and 14:31). Likewise, husbands aren't given the authority to "rule" unilaterally over their wives and households. They are to submit to the principles laid out in Scripture, which include meekness, mercy, gentleness, and self-denial. As Paul instructed the believers at Philippi, "in humility count others more significant than yourselves" (Phil. 2:3, ESV).

Third, *a husband's authority over his wife is not absolute.* A wife's ultimate allegiance, just like her husband's, is to God. This means that whatever leadership her husband extends over the home is limited to what is good and pleasing to God. In other words, if a husband wants his wife to do something that is clearly immoral or unethical, she can echo the words of Peter in Acts 5:29, "We must obey God rather than men" (ESV).

One reason that biblical submission is such an explosive topic is that many husbands have not exercised the servant-leadership that Scripture commands. I hope that Christian men, myself included, will take this as a challenge. What if we demonstrated Christ's self-sacrificial love so well that our neighbors didn't recoil from the biblical blueprint for marriage but desired it for themselves?

MAKING SENSE OF IT ALL

In his book *The Meaning of Marriage*, the pastor Timothy Keller puts it bluntly: Marriage is "like a riddle, a puzzle, a maze. It's not a Hallmark card."[8] But wait—I like Hallmark cards, don't you? Shouldn't we strive for the picture-perfect, happily-ever-after union? Is Dr. Keller just a killjoy? On the contrary, I think he's trying to make the point that marriage is a mystery—and the mystery of marriage revolves around the Gospel. In other words, if you want to understand marriage, if you want to have a thriving marriage, you first have to understand what Jesus of Nazareth did for you on the cross at Calvary.

Christianity is the only major religion in the world whose "boss" suffered and died at the hands of wicked men. In all other faiths, followers try to attain salvation through good behavior—in essence, paying the price for the ultimate reward. In other religions, "god" is many layers removed. Yet in Christianity, God became man, suffered, and paid our debt so that we might receive the reward of eternal life and unbroken fellowship with Him.

Christianity is full of paradoxes. The Apostle Paul reminds us that in Christ we are rich despite our poverty, that while lacking material abundance we possess every good and necessary thing (2 Cor. 6:10). And Christ Himself tells us that "whoever would save his life will lose it, but whoever loses his life for my sake will find it" (Matt. 16:25, ESV). The Christian understanding of marriage—indissoluble, built on self-sacrifice—is therefore paradoxical as well. It's a reflection of Christ's own sacrifice, in which He died that we might rise to eternal life.

THE DIVINE SECRET IS DISCLOSED

Reflecting on the mystery of marriage and its true purpose, the theologian George Knight III has written:

> Unbeknownst to the people of Moses' day, marriage was designed by God from the beginning to be a picture or parable of the relationship between Christ and the church. Back when God was planning what marriage would be like, He planned it for this great purpose: it would give a beautiful earthly picture of the relationship that would someday come about between Christ and His church. This was not known to people for many generations, and that is why Paul can call it a "mystery." But now in the New Testament age Paul reveals this mystery, and it is amazing.

> This means that when Paul wanted to tell the Ephesians about marriage, he did not just hunt around for a helpful analogy and suddenly think that "Christ and the church" might be a good teaching illustration. No, it was much more fundamental than that: Paul saw that when God designed the original marriage He already had Christ and the church in mind. This is one of God's great purposes in marriage: to picture the relationship between Christ and His redeemed people forever![9]

John Piper, a well-known pastor and theologian, agrees with Knight, adding that "marriage is a mystery—it contains and conceals a meaning far greater than what we see on the outside."[10] I think I know what he means. Each evening as I drive down the winding road toward my home, I pass house after house, the lights of each one shining invitingly through the trees. But only one house captures my attention—my own. Why? Because I know what's inside, and what's inside means all the world to me.

It's my hope and prayer that this book will help you appreciate more deeply the mystery that the institution of marriage represents and the sacredness of the particular union between you and your spouse. If you've lost that sense of miracle, mystery, and wonder, it's not too late to recover what the years may have obscured. After all, the Maker of marriage itself says, "Behold, I make all things new" (Rev. 21:15, ESV).

CHAPTER TWO

From Safety Seeker to Soul Mate

The conversion of courtly love into romantic monogamous love was largely the work of English, and even of Puritan, poets.[1]

—C. S. Lewis

Elizabeth Gilbert's bestselling memoir *Eat, Pray, Love: One Woman's Search for Everything across Italy, India, and Indonesia* chronicles her travels around the world in the wake of a painful divorce.[2] The highly anticipated sequel, *Committed: A Skeptic Makes Peace with Marriage*, tells of her decision to marry a Brazilian boyfriend, José Nunes, after realizing it was the easiest path to keep him legally in the country.[3] She writes, "The ambivalence wasn't 'Should I get married?' That was a given. The ambivalence was all around how do you do this without feeling like you're being forcibly marched into a form that's obsolete, that's politically disadvantageous to women in the extreme, that has an egregious history of injustice and misery and that you personally have a horrible history of misery with? Is there a little spot in there where you can rest at ease, and how do you find it?"[4]

Hardly an enthusiastic advocate for the institution of marriage, Ms. Gilbert acknowledges her ambivalence about marrying for the second time. Prior to meeting Mr. Nunes, she told the *New York Times*, "[I] careened from one intimate entanglement to the next—dozens of them—without so much as a day off between romances." She went on to admit, "Seduction was never a casual sport for me; it was more like a heist, adrenalizing and urgent. I would plan the heist for months, scouting out the target, looking for unguarded entries. Then I would break into his deepest vault, steal all his emotional currency and spend it on myself."[5]

Does that sound extreme? Ms. Gilbert's struggles are mirrored in the lives of many of those who turn to us at Focus on the Family. Our counselors call it serial monogamy—the practice of going from one romantic relationship to another. It's almost as if people who struggle with this habit are afraid to be alone—which is exactly what we find when they begin to open up.

The famed movie producer Arnon Milchan once quipped, "I was first married for ten years and had three children; then I lived together with my girlfriend for 12 years, and now I am with Amanda for three and a half years. I am a one-woman man."[6] Neurologists confirm the allure of this lifestyle, noting that when presented with a new relationship, the brain releases a satisfying cocktail of adrenaline, dopamine, and serotonin. In other words, for some, the thrill of all things new can be addictive. We're easily bored with the predictable.

Despite Elizabeth Gilbert's reputation for eloquent and even romantic prose, she adopts an almost clinical tone in evaluating her relationship with Mr. Nunes:

> My love affair with [José Nunes] had a wonderful element of romance to it, which I will always cherish. But it was not

> an infatuation, and here's how I can tell: because I did not demand that he become my Great Emancipator or my Source of All Life, nor did I immediately vanish into that man's chest cavity like a twisted, unrecognizable, parasitical homunculus. During our long period of courtship, I remained intact within my own personality, and I allowed myself to meet [him] for who he was.[7]

Ms. Gilbert, perhaps unknowingly, is actually getting at something quite healthy. That's because our ultimate identity and value must be rooted in our relationship with God, not our spouse.

If we expect our wife or husband to meet all our needs, we're going to be chronically miserable. I learned this early on in my own marriage. After our honeymoon, my wife and I traveled the country in a van, speaking at high schools, encouraging students to steer clear of drugs. It was a fun assignment, especially for a "people person" like me. But Jean is an introvert. Although she enjoyed the travel and adventure, the constant conversation and togetherness began to take their toll on her. One afternoon, she announced she was headed to the market for some groceries. I asked to go along. That was the last straw. "I love you," she assured me. "But I'd really like to take a break, get a breather. If you don't mind, I'd like to go alone." I was initially hurt, but I later discovered that though people and events energize me, they drain Jean. She recharges her batteries when she's alone.

Looking back, I see I was madly in love (and still am), but I enjoyed the affirmation and status that came with having a wife by my side. I'm also a talker and thrive on the constant flow of lively conversation. But too much of anything—even togetherness in marriage—isn't necessarily a good thing. I was smothering her! I've since learned to give her space, and our marriage is better for it.

My friend Graham, a pastor, understands this. When he was a boy, he desperately wanted a border collie—until his parents convinced him to do some research. "I quickly discovered," he recalls in a sermon, "that they need lots of room to roam. The worst thing you can do for a border collie is to put it in a tiny apartment. You know what happens to border collies that get cooped up? They get easily aggravated. They start to bite. They become mean. They will nip at your heels every time you come in. That's a lot like marriages. Couples who are struggling are often, believe it or not, *too* close. It's unhealthy to be so entirely insulated that you begin to lose a bit of your identity." Jean Daly would certainly agree.

THE HISTORY OF MARRIAGE

Only a Pollyanna would deny that the institution of marriage is in serious trouble. Fewer people get married these days, and those who do are marrying later in life. The average age for a first-time marriage today is 28.3 for men and 25.8 for women; in 1960 it was 23 and 20, respectively.[8] Cohabitation rates are soaring. According Dr. Bradford Wilcox, a scholar of marriage, "Since the 1960s, the rate of new marriages has fallen by more than 50 percent, and rates of divorce and single parenthood have more than doubled."[9]

But are things really as bleak as the statistics suggest? To borrow a phrase from Paul Harvey, in times like these, it is wise to remember there have always been times like these. In the 1920s and 1930s, worried Americans were buying books titled *The Marriage Crisis*, *Family Disorganization*, and *Marriage at the Crossroads*. One newspaper commentator lamented, "The lack of marital harmony in this country is largely due to the high strain of modern living. . . ."[10] Sound familiar? The conventional wisdom about marriage is that the wheels began falling off only recently, but the evidence suggests otherwise. So what was causing this anxiety nearly a century ago?

Sociologists suggest that marriage was undergoing a cataclysmic shift at the turn of the twentieth century because America itself was changing dramatically. The industrial revolution turned the business of America into, well, business. Prior to the twentieth century, American society was largely agrarian, husbands and wives working side by side on the farm, the rural environment shaping their relationship.[11] Many of the traits that resulted in a profitable farm, such as teamwork and a sacrificial spirit among its workers, are also keys to a successful marriage. Working together in the fields prepared couples for a lifetime of marital harmony. The sociologist Paul R. Amato concludes:

> During this era marriage was essential to the welfare of individual family members and the larger community. Before the development of specialized services and institutions, family members relied on each other to meet a wide range of needs, including child care, economic production, job training, and elder care. Because cohesive families were necessary for survival, the entire community had an interest in ensuring marital stability.[12]

Times change, but the community still needs marital stability. Scholars have documented the devastating costs of marital instability:

- Children with divorced parents are more likely to be victims of abuse.
- These children also have more health, behavioral, and emotional problems, which can contribute to higher rates of drug and alcohol addiction. They also have higher rates of suicide than children with married parents.
- Children of divorced parents also suffer setbacks in school, performing worse in reading, spelling, and math. They repeat grades and even drop out at higher

rates than their peers, and they have lower rates of college graduation.
- Divorce also has financial costs. Among families with children, income can drop by as much as 50 percent after a divorce, even if these families were not poor to begin with. Nearly half of parents with children who are going through a divorce fall into poverty.
- Participation in religious worship decreases after parents divorce, which means kids miss out on the benefits associated with regular religious practice, including better health, longer marriages, and better family life.[13]

But the scholars are just telling me what I already know. When my own father abandoned our family when I was five years old, our world fell apart. The late Southern novelist Pat Conroy may have said it best—"every divorce is the death of a small civilization."[14] We quickly fell into poverty. My mother was forced to work full-time as a waitress to make ends meet. Not only did I stop seeing my father regularly, but my mom was not home in the afternoons and evenings. I was off to school before she woke up. That was our routine. Did my mom and dad marry for stability or love? I was too young to ask. I'd like to think they married for both. They tried, but my father just couldn't resist alcohol.

Looking back on my parents' marriage, I don't think they spent much time considering God's grand design for the institution. Neither of them was a believer, although my mom accepted Christ just prior to her death from cancer. They were drifting, hoping to keep things together. They weren't alone then, nor would they be in the minority today. If we're honest with ourselves, we have to acknowledge that most of us are drifting through our lives and marriages, simply reacting to the next thing that happens to us. We don't invest in analyzing our own marriage, let alone the history of the institution itself.

Of course, the first marriage was in the Garden of Eden between Adam and Eve. But the sociological evidence of marriage dates back more than four thousand years to Mesopotamia. In his landmark study *The History of Human Marriage*, the sociologist Edward Westermarck observed, "That the functions of the husband and father in the family are not merely of the sexual and procreative kind, but involve the duty of protecting the wife and children, is testified by an array of facts relating to people in all quarters of the world and in all stages of civilization."[15] In other words, while marriage may differ in various ways across cultures—the number of spouses, the division of labor, and living arrangements—it has always been centered on the union of husband and wife and their common children.

Marriage is more than a private arrangement between the couple and their immediate families. It is an essential and irreplaceable public institution. Sociologists are in agreement that, with few exceptions, marriage historically has had less to do with "romantic love" than with social responsibility. It wasn't until the eighteenth-century Romantics began to write about marriage in sensual terms that most people thought of it as a source of emotional and sexual satisfaction. More often than not, couples married for security, not for "happily ever after."

LIBERATING OR DEPRESSING?

The evolution of marriage from an institution that provides safety into a union of soul mates helps explain, I think, the source of some of the classic frustrations between husbands and wives. If I may generalize, men tend to thrive when marriage is more about security than about romance. Early in our marriage, Jean would have preferred for me to be more romantic, sharing candlelit dinners with her and writing love letters that rival a Shakespearean sonnet. I'll admit that I could have been more thoughtful and responsive, but over time, Jean has come to appreciate that one of the ways I express my love for her is by providing stability in the home. But in our culture as a whole, the focus on romantic love has taken its toll. Gary Thomas writes eloquently about this problem: "Romantic love has no elasticity to it. It can never be stretched; it simply shatters. Mature love, the kind demanded of a good marriage, must stretch, as the sinful human condition is such that all of us bear conflicting conditions."[16]

Thomas goes on to pose a provocative but insightful question: What if marriage is more about our holiness than our happiness? Marriage is designed to transform our selfishness into selflessness. As the nineteenth-century English pastor George Hughes Hepworth once said, "The purpose of marriage is the building of the home. If there is any other motive—wealth or social position—we perform an act of sacrilege, defy the laws of the universe and reap a harvest of tears."[17] Do our actions measure up to this standard?

SOUL MATE SYNDROME

Do you believe in soul mates, the idea that there's one person in the world without whom your life would be incomplete? The poet Samuel Taylor Coleridge is credited with coining the phrase back in 1822. "To be happy in Married life," he wrote, "you must have a Soul-mate."[18] From the romance writer Faye Hall ("True love is finding your soul mate in your best friend"[19]) to Uncle Rico in the cult-favorite movie *Napoleon Dynamite* ("I'd be making millions of dollars and living in a big ol' mansion somewhere, soaking it up in a hot tub with my soul mate"), the belief is perpetuated everywhere. It makes for an entertaining Hollywood screenplay, but is it foolish to build a marriage on it? I think so.

Scholars suggest that the concept of the individual's incompleteness emanates from Plato's *Symposium*, a philosophic dialogue written between 385 and 380 BC, in which Aristophanes suggests that at one time, androgynous human beings had two faces, four legs, and four arms, the male and female joined in the same person. According to the legend, Zeus became jealous of man's happiness and divided everyone in half, stating, "I shall now cut each of them in two . . . and they will be both weaker and more useful to us through the increase in their numbers."[20] Thus divided, human beings spend their days in a search for their "other half"—in other words, their soul mate.

It all sounds kind of crazy, doesn't it? The Bible's explanation of man's quest for companionship is far more convincing. Indeed, it was the Lord Himself who declared, "It is not good for the man to be alone. I will make a helper suitable for him" (Gen. 2:18, NIV). Gary Thomas reflects on what really completes us and the kind of companionship singles should be searching for:

> According to the Bible, our problem is not that we've been sliced apart from an ancient human half but that we have been separated from God by our sin and need to be reconciled to God through the work of Jesus Christ on the cross. Once we are reconciled to God, He brings us together as humans. Marriage is a glorious reality, but it is secondary to our spiritual identity as children of God and something that won't even exist in heaven (Matthew 22:30). Our search for a life mate, then, isn't one of desperation, but rather one of patiently looking for someone with whom we can share God's love and live out God's purpose.[21]

We need to stop trying, he says, to make marriage something that it isn't designed to be, "perfect happiness, conflict-free living and idolatrous obsession. The problem with looking to another human to complete us is that spiritually speaking, it's idolatry. We are to find our fulfillment and purpose in God . . . and if we expect our spouse to be 'God' to us, he or she will fail every day. No person can live up to such expectations."[22]

The famously provocative theologian Stanley Hauerwas agrees:

> Destructive to marriage is the self-fulfillment ethic that assumes marriage and the family are primarily institutions of personal fulfillment, necessary for us to become "whole" and happy. The assumption is that there is someone just right for us to marry and that if we look closely enough we will find the right person. This moral assumption overlooks a crucial aspect to marriage. It fails to appreciate the fact that we always marry the wrong person.
>
> We never know whom we marry; we just think we do. Or even if we first marry the right person, just give it a while and he or she will change. For marriage, being [the enormous thing it is,] means we are not the same person after we have entered it. The primary challenge of marriage is learning how to love and care for the stranger to whom you find yourself married.[23]

It's jarring to think that after nearly thirty years I'm still married to "a stranger," but Hauerwas is right. Am I the same person Jean Stephens agreed to marry in 1986? Hardly. After all, if we're allowing the Holy Spirit to shape us, none of us should be the same person from one year to the next. The Apostle Paul had this process of sanctification in mind when he wrote, "As the Spirit of the Lord works within us, we become more and more like Him and reflect His glory even more" (2 Cor. 3:18, NLT). But how does this transformation happen in real life? "Through the choices we make," writes the pastor Rick Warren. "We choose to do the right thing in situations and then trust God's Spirit to give us his power, love, faith, and wisdom to do it. Since God's Spirit lives inside of us, these things are always available for the asking."[24] I have to lay down *my* wants and desires and ask the Holy Spirit to help me meet the desires and needs of my spouse. There's really no other way to do it.

CHAPTER THREE

Why Marry at All?

Marriage has the power to set the course of your life as a whole. If your marriage is strong, even if all the circumstances in your life around you are filled with trouble and weakness, it won't matter. You will be able to move out into the world in strength.[1]

—Timothy Keller

His name was Glynn "Scotty" Wolfe, and when he died in 1997 at the age of eighty-eight he held the *Guinness Book of World Records* title for the most times married—twenty-nine, to be exact.[2] Those closest to him described the Indiana native as an affable, flamboyant, "Bible-thumping" one-time Baptist minister who fell in and out of love quickly. Over the years he was referred to jokingly as a "mass marrier" and a "spouse-iopath." After marrying Helen, his first wife, in 1932, he said, "Everything was lovely. I realized right then and there that being married was the greatest thing in the world."

Yet months later he divorced Helen and married Marjorie. Then came Margie and later her girlfriend Mildred. Several of his marriages lasted mere months; most lasted only a couple of years. His final marriage, to Linda Essex, was reportedly a publicity stunt, with Linda hitting the *Guinness Book of World Records* mark as the most-married woman (twenty-three times). In the end, this man who claimed nineteen children and forty grandchildren died penniless in a nursing home. Initially, nobody stepped forward even to claim the body. None of his ex-wives attended his funeral.[3]

Glynn Wolfe's eccentric marital history could be dismissed as a case of good intentions gone wrong. After all, as he was preparing for his twenty-sixth marriage he reportedly declared, "I marry 'em for keeps."[4] When asked why he continued to get married despite his poor record of marital success, he said, "Marriage is like stamp collecting. You keep looking to find the rare one."[5]

It goes without saying that few people go into marriage expecting it to fail. Like Wolfe, we marry "for keeps." When the British actress Joan Collins divorced her fourth husband, she told the press, "I got married because I truly believed that this was a relationship that was going to last."[6] Hollywood legends Lana Turner, Mickey Rooney, Zsa Zsa Gabor, and Elizabeth Taylor, each of whom married eight times, made similar statements. The "next one" was going to be "the one." When someone asked Mickey Rooney at the end of his life if he would marry all of his wives again, he replied, "Absolutely. I loved every one of them."[7]

The talk show host Larry King is also on his eighth marriage. His childhood friend Herbie Cohen once observed that "Larry is in love with being in love. If Larry loved someone, instead of sleeping with her, which would be the way most people would handle those situations, Larry married her."[8] Larry's brother, Marty Zeiger, adds, "The multiple marriages can be explained in part by what happens when tradition meets impetuousness and restlessness. It was leap before you look."[9]

Before I delve more deeply into the question of why we should marry at all, I'd like to address the issue of premarital sex, to which Marty Zeiger alludes. Years ago, marrying a female you were already sexually involved with was referred to as "making an honest woman of her." Marrying to morally legitimize sexual relations is rooted in good intentions, but it shouldn't be a Christian's only motive. The Scriptures clearly state that sex is for marriage and marriage is for sex (Gen. 1:27, 2:24; Matt. 19:4–5). That's because sex is not a form of casual recreation, merely a pleasurable way of expressing mutual love. It's how two persons become one flesh. God wants us to reserve sex for marriage not because it's "bad" or "dirty" but precisely because of its unique and wonderful purpose.

Sex is a holy mystery, a powerful bonding agent that shapes and affects the relationship between a man and a woman as nothing else can. To take it outside of marriage is like using the wine consecrated for Holy Communion for a frat house drinking party. We'll dive deeper into the subject of intimacy within the confines of marriage later, but marrying for the sole purpose of legitimizing our sexual enjoyment undermines the institution of marriage itself. Yes—the Apostle Paul wrote, "If they cannot exercise self-control, they should marry. For it is better to marry than to burn with passion" (1 Cor. 7:9, ESV), but I don't believe he was suggesting that we should reduce the institution of marriage to a tool to control lust.

This question may be of no interest to non-Christian readers, but if you're a committed Christian who desires sexual intimacy, please hear me. Running down the aisle simply to feel less guilty about hopping into bed with your girlfriend or boyfriend is not wise. As we'll see, there are many factors to consider in choosing a spouse, and it might surprise you to hear that sexual compatibility, in my view, is not among the most important.

A SECULAR CASE FOR MARRIAGE

Although experts believe that the record-low marriage rate in the United States bottomed out in 2015 (6.74 per 1,000 people),[10] the downward trend still remains a cause for great concern because of the sheer numbers of those affected. It's also troublesome because it's not as if Americans have given up on romantic relationships. Instead of getting married, couples are simply living together. Even among Christians, twenty- and thirty-something men and women have grown sour on marriage, choosing to move in together unwed, taking one another on a "test drive." No wedding, no ring, and, presumably, no worries. If it doesn't work out (and chances are it won't), well, "no harm, no foul." But there is *always* harm from a moral and spiritual perspective and often from other perspectives as well.

A lot of emotion is wrapped up in this topic. I realize some of my readers are living together outside of marriage. Or perhaps you have adult children who are currently doing so. It's not my intention to demean anyone. I hope that a loving and candid discussion about it will help you see that God's plan for marriage provides all of us with the best chance to thrive as families.

Consider the changes of the past fifty years. In the early 1960s, there were fewer than five hundred thousand unmarried couples living together in the United States.[11] By 2011, according to the U.S. Census Bureau, that number had skyrocketed to 7.6 million opposite-sex cohabiting couples and over five hundred thousand same-sex couples living together.[12] Data from the Centers for Disease Control and Prevention confirm that since the mid-1980s marriage has been declining at a much steeper rate than at any other time in our history.[13]

Despite this unprecedented downward trajectory of the modern marriage rate, the case for marriage is still being made in the most surprising of places. For example, *Cosmopolitan* magazine, hardly a mouthpiece for the traditional point of view, offers seven perfectly sound reasons for tying the knot:

- Marriage makes your relationship more meaningful.
- It makes your relationship more likely to last.
- It makes you feel and act like a team.
- It gives you a feeling of rootedness and calm.
- It shows your partner how important he is to you.
- There are financial and other practical benefits to marriage.
- You'll have a better sex life.[14]

As the *Cosmo* article suggests, secular research actually validates biblical truth. The scientific studies of the past few decades show that God's blueprint for the family leads to human flourishing. Millions of people focus on diet, exercise, supplements, relaxation, and medications to improve their health, but researchers have discovered that one of the most powerful predictors of good health and well-being is *marriage*. One sociologist has suggested that marriage improves your health as much as giving up smoking.

Married adults are more likely to recognize symptoms of illness, seek medical treatment, avoid risky behavior, recover quickly, and eat a healthy diet than their unmarried counterparts, and so they live longer.[15] No one has the same interest in your health that your spouse does, and no one watches after you as he or she does. In case you haven't noticed, wives tend to discourage drinking, smoking, unnecessary risk taking, and unhealthy eating. In fact, men start giving up their self-destructive behavior up to a year before their actual wedding date. It seems that even *planning* to get married improves a man's health. The emotional support of a spouse can help you recover from both minor and major illnesses more quickly and cope with chronic diseases. Some studies suggest that marital relationships actually boost the immune system, making sickness less likely in the first place.

Marriage is good for your mental health as well. Married people have substantially lower rates of severe depression and are at least half as likely to develop a psychiatric disorder as never-married, cohabiting, or divorced persons.[16] Men in nations with higher rates of marriage are happier than men in nations with lower rates of marriage. Some researchers have compared the overall increased happiness experienced by the married to the boost experienced after receiving a hundred-thousand-dollar annual pay raise.[17]

The research is clear, diverse, and consistent. Those who marry live longer and are more likely to be healthy and happy. In fact, according to a study at the University of Rochester, a person in a happy marriage is likely to live longer after heart surgery than someone who is single or unhappy in his marriage. "I can only imagine that people who have a good marriage are pretty happy people," said a Boston cardiac surgeon, Robert Hagberg. "So they don't have many destructive behavior patterns—they don't drink, they don't smoke, they don't stay out late trying to pick up dates."[18]

COULD IT BE THAT THE NEWS ISN'T AS BAD AS IT SEEMS?

I frequently come across articles by pundits or even sociologists suggesting that marriage is hurdling toward obsolescence, citing the same statistics I have cited. It's true that marriage and family trends have been headed in the wrong direction for some time. Almost every indicator that should be up is down, and nearly every indicator that should be down is up. Only the divorce rate has stabilized, and it's still above 40 percent. Still, to suggest that marriage is on the verge of obsolescence doesn't quite square with the opinions of the very people who account for its future standing.

According to a Pew survey released in 2014, 60 percent of American adults cohabiting with a significant other desire to wed eventually, while only 16 percent of them express no interest at all in tying the knot.[19] In fact, Pew's data show that more people want to marry today than did in 2007.[20] Believe it or not, more Americans believe the sun revolves around the earth (18 percent) than say they have absolutely no desire ever to marry (13 percent).

The results of Pew's secular research even contain some good news for Christians. Seventy-six percent of the respondents indicated that their own family was "the most important element" in life, while 22 percent said it was "one of the most import elements."[21] Nevertheless, there remains a nagging question: Why the disparity between what people say they believe about marriage and how they act?

It turns out that the disparity between belief and behavior is not new. Colonial America was rife with cohabitation. In his book *Sexual Revolution in Early America*, Richard Godbeer quotes a clergyman who was appalled at the prevalence of sex outside marriage in the province of New York in 1695. "[M]any couples live together without ever being married in any manner or way," the minister complained, outraged at the "ante-nuptial fornication" which was "not looked upon as any scandal or sin."[22]

Today, even the most casual observer of marriage would acknowledge that the institution is too often held in low esteem. From television to movies to music, the bonds of matrimony, which God gives to man as an anchor of stability, are despised as confining chains. Since the Church is only as healthy as its most unhealthy people, we too bear blame. Have we not often been more inclined to focus on the challenges of marriage than on its joys? When the divorce rate within the Church is nearly as bad as the divorce rate outside of it, we must take a hard and honest look at ourselves.

Christians have to be humble, recognizing that the Apostle Paul gave perhaps the best explanation for why personal belief does not always square with personal behavior—"all have sinned and fall short of the glory of God" (Rom. 3:23, ESV). Acknowledging that "I do not do the good I want, but the evil I do not want is what I keep on doing" (Rom. 7:19, ESV), Paul expressed a major challenge facing those inside and outside the Church. Most people want to get married, but for any number of reasons—pessimism, fear, perceived convenience—many of them do not. Nevertheless, that they want to marry at all is an important and positive sign.

THE GOOD NEWS

Designed as a gift to mankind that brings glory to the Creator, marriage is critical to the sustainability and stability of society. Although fewer people are choosing to marry, marriage will never be obsolete because God has built into every human being a desire for companionship, a craving to love and be loved. I believe this built-in desire is driving the rise in cohabitation. It reminds me of the seventeenth-century mathematician and philosopher Blaise Pascal's observation:

> What else does this craving, and this helplessness, proclaim but that there was once in man a true happiness, of which all that now remains is the empty print and trace? This he tries in vain to fill with everything around him, seeking in things that are not there the help he cannot find in those that are, though none can help, since this infinite abyss can be filled only with an infinite and immutable object; in other words by God himself.[23]

I can certainly relate. Can you? Although I was a Christian during my undergraduate days, I spent long stretches of time reading my textbooks but not my Bible. I was caught up in the things of this world. The heart of someone who lacks a personal relationship with Jesus Christ is constantly searching. There's a void that needs to be filled. It's easy to see how that need, combined with the recklessness of youth, leads us into trouble in our personal and romantic relationships.

The public opinion researcher David Kinnaman observes that persons aged sixteen to twenty-nine are engaged in a "nearly constant search for fresh experiences and new sources of motivation,"[24] leaving them vulnerable to addictions and more likely to engage in extreme behavior. It's all an attempt to fill the void and to find what God made us for. As the Scottish novelist Bruce Marshall memorably put it, "The young man who rings the bell at the brothel is unconsciously looking for God."[25]

David Popenoe, a sociologist and co-director of the National Marriage Project, has suggested that those who say marriage is becoming obsolete might be voicing a fear, not expressing a wish.[26] He has touched on something profound. If you ask people what they fear the most, they'll tell you terrorism, death, pain, and even public speaking and spiders. Yet if you speak more intimately with them—or even observe how they live—you often get a very different take on what truly burdens them.

Since God created man for companionship, it makes sense that many of us fear loneliness most of all. Studies have confirmed that loneliness is on the rise in America, even as we're increasingly connected technologically. By some estimates, sixty million Americans—20 percent of the population—are chronically lonely,[27] and many of them have absolutely nobody with whom to talk over important or intimate matters.

No wonder so many fear the loss of marriage as an institution. If there is no marriage, there is no hope of that long walk into the sunset with your aging spouse by your side. Ronald Reagan, whose love affair with his beloved Nancy has been so well chronicled, perfectly captured what we long for in marriage: "Nancy's power was the power of, well, giving me a marriage that was like an adolescent's dream of what marriage should be. Clark Gable had some words once, when he said there is nothing more wonderful for a man than to know as he approaches his own doorstep that someone on the other side of that door is listening for the sound of his footsteps."[28]

Even while he was president, Mr. Reagan used to stand by the window in the White House and watch for the lights of the car that would be bringing his Nancy home. I can relate. I travel quite a bit in my role at Focus on the Family and have grown accustomed to the rhythm of life on the road. In fact, I'm usually so busy that I don't have time to be lonely. But when I'm home and Jean's traveling, it's entirely different. I miss her terribly and find myself counting the hours until her return. In those (fortunately) rare moments I appreciate her companionship all the more, and my convictions about the sanctity of marriage are renewed. Indeed, all Christians are called to preserve this God-ordained institution and share with their neighbors its benefits and His ultimate reasons for it.

Many of our citizens fear the loss of marriage because they've never seen it modeled well in their own families or communities. We would be wise, then, to show them marriage as it was intended to be. Marriage will never be obsolete, because God has wired into our hearts a desire to be for another. And isn't it telling that God's narrative begins with a marriage in the Garden of Eden and ends with the wedding feast of the Lamb? In fact, Jesus's own public ministry on earth began at the wedding at Cana. Theologians suggest these three high points in history are all marked by covenant love, a bond that cannot be broken.

We have a story to tell—the story of man's longing to give himself to another and to receive the other's gift of self, the story of the gift of God that satisfies that longing in a holy lifelong partnership. We will show that marriage can never be obsolete but is a timeless treasure to be respected and protected.

CHAPTER FOUR

Reformed and Transformed

The central problem of every society is to define appropriate roles for men.[1]

—Margaret Mead

Early one morning, before the sun broke the horizon and the busyness of the day took hold, our youngest son, Troy, joined me in our living room. I often prepare for the coming day in my chair over coffee there, reviewing prep for my daily radio broadcast. I also like to read or listen to the Bible, answer e-mails, and catch up on correspondence with family and friends. But on this particular day, Troy and I were talking about what makes a man. We discussed the classic characteristics of manhood, diving into such traits as personal and societal responsibility, good manners, kindness, sexual discipline, and courageous living, to name just a few.

Hoping to instigate a deeper conversation, I posed a question: "What does it mean to be courageous?" Without missing a beat, he replied, "Courage is being scared to death but saddling up anyway."

"Where did you come up with that one?" I responded, impressed with his wit.

"It's the quote on your coffee mug," he answered with a sly smile. "John Wayne." Troy is too young to have an appreciation for the man whom the *New York Times* once described as "a symbolic male figure, a man of impregnable virility and the embodiment of simplistic, laconic virtues, packaged in a well-built, 6-foot-4-inch, 225-pound frame."[2] But the quotation on my coffee mug made sense to him.

John Wayne's reputation for courage is based, of course, on fictional Hollywood roles. Only those closest to him would know how close that reputation was to reality. We do know that Marion Morrison (his real name) wasn't as successful in his personal life as John Wayne was on the screen. After two divorces, he married Pilar Pallette in 1954. They struggled throughout their twenty-nine-year marriage and eventually separated. Thankfully, various accounts suggest that John Wayne experienced a dramatic conversion to Christianity just prior to his death in 1979.

That exchange about courage and John Wayne led Troy and me into a conversation about masculinity and its role in marriage. It's an important topic. Marriages often fail because of confusion about true manhood.

Grown men are responsible for their own actions, but so many of us grew up with fathers who failed to show us what being a man is all about. My own father, in his drunken rages, would threaten my mother and scare the living daylights out of me. He walked out on us when I was just five, floating in and out of my life for years, regularly breaking promises, and ultimately disappointing me.

Was I destined to follow in my father's footsteps with my own children? Statistically speaking, yes. Studies indicate that the vast majority of us parent the way we were parented. Fortunately, several influential men (mostly athletic coaches) stepped into my life and provided that much-needed mentor role for me. I found the Lord in high school, and the trajectory of my life slowly began to turn. The chain of dysfunction was broken. To this day, I do my best to give our boys what I so terribly missed in my own childhood—the unconditional love of a father and the comfort of knowing that I'll never leave them, no matter what happens. It hasn't been easy, and I envy my friends who share stories of their idyllic boyhood, of hunting and fishing with their fathers. The closest I ever got to that scene was on television.

REAL MANHOOD

So if a husband's biblical masculinity is a key to a great marriage, what does it mean to be a man after God's own heart? Our popular culture depicts masculinity in the extremes. The typical man is either a bumbling goofball, the beer-guzzling buffoon who regularly loses the recipe for ice, or a testosterone-crazed warrior with an illegal arsenal in the basement, the tactless bore who sexually exploits women for his own pleasure. In contrast with this counterfeit masculinity, my friend Robert Lewis, the bestselling author of *Raising a Modern-Day Knight*,[3] identifies four principles of authentic biblical manhood, each of which is perfectly modeled in the life of Jesus:

1. A true man rejects passivity.
2. A true man accepts the three responsibilities God gives him: a will to obey, a work to do, and a woman to love.
3. A true man leads courageously.
4. A true man invests eternally—that is, he lives not for the moment but for eternity.

This ideal of Christian manhood comes to life in C. S. Lewis's *Chronicles of Narnia.* Throughout those seven tales, true masculinity is depicted as graceful and gentle yet strong and fierce, especially in battle. It's not an either-or proposition but the perfect blend of the two. As someone once told me, show me strength and power without tenderness and I'll show you a brute. Show me gentleness with power and I'll show you a true man.

THE LESSONS OF SEPTEMBER 11

Shortly after the terrorist attacks of September 11, 2001, Peggy Noonan, a former speechwriter for Ronald Reagan who lives in New York City, wrote a poignant essay for the *Wall Street Journal* about a resurgence of masculinity that she noticed throughout the metropolitan area. She titled it "Welcome Back, Duke."[4] And although she wasn't intending to write about men and marriage, she inevitably did just that. With her permission, I'd like to share a portion of what she wrote:

> Men are back. A certain style of manliness is once again being honored and celebrated in our country since September 11. You might say it suddenly emerged from the rubble of the past quarter century, and emerged when a certain kind of man came forth to get our great country out of the fix it was in.
>
> I am speaking of masculine men, men who push things and pull things and haul things and build things, men who charge up the stairs in a hundred pounds of gear and tell everyone else where to go to be safe. Men who are welders, who do construction, men who are cops and firemen. They are all of them, one way or another, the men who put the

fire out, the men who are digging the rubble out, and the men who will build whatever takes its place.

And their style is back in style. We are experiencing a new respect for their old-fashioned masculinity, a new respect for physical courage, for strength and for the willingness to use both for the good of others.

You didn't have to be a fireman to be one of the manly men of September 11. Those businessmen on flight 93, which was supposed to hit Washington, the businessmen who didn't live by their hands or their backs but who found out what was happening to their country, said goodbye to the people they loved, snapped the cell phone shut and said, "Let's roll." Those were tough men, the ones who forced that plane down in Pennsylvania. They were tough, brave guys.

Let me tell you when I first realized what I'm saying. On Friday, September 14, I went with friends down to the staging area on the West Side Highway where all the trucks filled with guys coming off a twelve-hour shift at ground zero would pass by. They were tough, rough men, the grunts of the city—construction workers and electrical workers and cops and emergency medical workers and firemen.

I joined a group that was just standing there as the truck convoys went by. And all we did was cheer. We all wanted to do some kind of volunteer work but there was nothing left to do, so we stood and cheered those who were doing. The trucks would go by and we'd cheer and wave and shout "God bless you!" and "We love you!" We waved flags and signs, clapped and threw kisses, and we meant it: *We loved these men.* And as the workers would go by—they would wave to us from their trucks and buses, and smile and nod—I realized that a lot of them were men who hadn't been applauded since the day they danced to their song with their bride at the wedding.

And suddenly I looked around me at all of us who were cheering. And saw who we were. Investment bankers! Orthodontists! Magazine editors! In my group, a lawyer, a columnist and a writer. We had been the kings and queens of the city, respected professionals in a city that respects its professional class. And this night we were nobody. We were so useless, all we could do was applaud the somebodies, the workers who, unlike us, had not been applauded much in their lives.

And now they were saving our city.

I turned to my friend and said, "I have seen the grunts of New York become kings and queens of the City." I was so moved and, oddly I guess, grateful. Because they'd always been the people who ran the place, who kept it going, they'd just never been given their due. But now—"And the last shall be first"—we were making up for it.

It may seem that I am really talking about class—the professional classes have a new appreciation for the working class men of Lodi, N.J., or Astoria, Queens. But what I'm attempting to talk about is actual manliness, which often seems tied up with class issues, as they say, but isn't always by any means the same thing.

Here's what I'm trying to say: Once about ten years ago there was a story—you might have read it in your local tabloid, or a supermarket tabloid like the *National Enquirer*—about an American man and woman who were on their honeymoon in Australia or New Zealand. They were swimming in the ocean, the water chest-high. From nowhere came a shark. The shark went straight for the woman, opened its jaws. Do you know what the man did? He punched the shark in the head. He punched it and punched it again. He did not do brilliant commentary on the shark, he did not share his sensitive feelings about the shark, he did not make wry observations about the shark, he punched the shark in the head. So the shark let go of his wife and went straight for him. And it killed him. The wife survived to tell the story of what her husband had done. He had tried to deck the shark. I told my friends: That's what a wonderful man is, a man who will try to deck the shark.

I don't know what the guy did for a living, but he had a very old-fashioned sense of what it is to be a man, and I think that sense is coming back into style because of who saved us on September 11, and that is very good for our country.

Why? Well, manliness wins wars. Strength and guts plus brains and spirit wins wars. But also, you know what follows manliness? The gentleman. The return of manliness will bring a return of gentlemanliness, for a simple reason: masculine men are almost by definition gentlemen. Example: If you're a woman and you go to a faculty meeting at an Ivy League university you'll have to fight with a male intellectual for a chair, but I assure you that if you go to a Knights of Columbus hall, the men inside (cops, firemen, insurance agents) will rise to offer you a seat. Because they are manly men, and gentlemen.

It is hard to be a man. I am certain of it; to be a man in this world is not easy. I know you are thinking, *But it's not easy to be a woman*, and you are so right. But women get to complain and make others feel bad about their plight. Men have to suck it up. Good men suck it up and remain good-natured, constructive and helpful; less-good men become the kind of men who are spoofed on "The Man Show"—babe-watching, dope-smoking nihilists. (Nihilism is not manly, it is the last refuge of sissies.)

I should discuss how manliness and its brother, gentlemanliness, went out of style. I know, because I was there. In fact, I may have done it. I remember exactly when: It was in the mid-'70s, and I was in my mid-20s, and a big, nice, middle-aged man got up from his seat to help me haul a big piece of luggage into the overhead luggage space on a plane. I was a feminist, and knew our rules and rants. "I can do it myself," I snapped.

It was important that he know women are strong. It was even more important, it turns out, that I know I was a jackass, but I didn't. I embarrassed a nice man who was attempting to help a lady. I wasn't lady enough to let him. I bet he never offered to help a lady again. I bet he became an intellectual, or a writer, and not a good man like a fireman or a businessman who says, "Let's roll."

But perhaps it wasn't just me. I was there in America, as a child, when John Wayne was a hero, and a symbol of American manliness. He was strong, and silent. And I was there in America when they killed John Wayne by a thousand cuts. A lot of people killed him—not only feminists but peaceniks, leftists, intellectuals, others. You could even say it was Woody Allen who did it, through laughter and an endearing admission of his own nervousness and fear. He made nervousness and fearfulness the admired style. He made not being able to deck the shark, but doing the funniest commentary on not decking the shark, seem...cool.

> But when we killed John Wayne, you know who we were left with. We were left with John Wayne's friendly-antagonist sidekick in the old John Ford movies, Barry Fitzgerald. The small, nervous, gossiping neighborhood commentator Barry Fitzgerald, who wanted to talk about everything and do nothing.
>
> This was not progress. It was not improvement.
>
> I missed John Wayne.
>
> But now I think...he's back. I think he returned on September 11. I think he ran up the stairs, threw the kid over his back like a sack of potatoes, came back down and shoveled rubble. I think he's in Afghanistan now, saying, with his slow swagger and simmering silence, "Yer in a whole lotta trouble now, Osama-boy."
>
> I think he's back in style. And none too soon.
>
> Welcome back, Duke.

Of course, many of these same men that Ms. Noonan wrote about still exist. They're in the firehouses, police cruisers, classrooms, markets, and sidelines of America's playing fields. They should also be in the homes on your street, loving their wives and nurturing and raising their kids.

SHOULD WE BE RAISING NICE GUYS?

After the attention given to the patriotism and masculine grit of September 11 began to subside, I noticed another, less encouraging trend. It's a call to raise boys not to be tough men who race into burning buildings but to be "nice guys." Nowadays men are expected to be sweet and gentle—almost feminine—an expectation that is putting the future of marriage at risk. We don't need more "nice guys." We need strong men.

First of all, let me clarify. If by "nice guys," we mean men of true character, then I'm all for that. We need guys who treat their wives with love and respect and emotionally engage with their children. The "nice guys" we could use fewer of are men who have crossed the line from thoughtfulness to the passivity that Robert Lewis warns about. Passive men overlook problems instead of facing them. Maybe you know guys like this. They rarely get angry or show passion for anything. At first you think it's because they're so in control of their emotions, but when you get to know them, you realize they're simply indifferent. They lack the strength and courage to stand up against injustice or to support those in need.

Frankly, our families and our culture can't afford that weakness. Men ought to be gentle and nurturing with their wives and children, but when it's time to protect and defend what matters, they should show their strength. Paul Coughlin defines masculinity as "love bolstered by courage." That virtue was abundantly evident in Jesus. When others were cold-hearted, He was tender and compassionate. When others were cowardly, Jesus was as bold as a lion. Masculinity isn't tender *or* tough. It's tender *and* tough. It's why we need men of courage, not "nice guys."

TIME TO "MAN UP"?

You've probably heard the catchphrase "man up!" but what does it mean anymore? Writing about modern masculinity, Al Mohler has this to say:

> A true masculinity is grounded in a man's determination to fulfill his manhood in being a good husband, father, citizen, worker, leader, and friend—one who makes a difference, fulfills a role for others, and devotes his life to these tasks. Most of our fathers went to work early and toiled all

> day because they knew it was their duty to put bread on the table, a roof over our heads, and a future in front of us. They made their way to ball games and school events dead tired, went home and took care of things, and then got up and did it all over again the next day.[5]

Comparing yesterday's fathers with today's, Dr. Mohler warns: "Today's men are likely to be more nurturing, but they are also statistically less faithful. They may be changing more diapers, but they are also more likely to change spouses. Men must be encouraged and expected to be both faithful fathers and faithful husbands. Otherwise, any society is in big trouble."[6]

How can we help those who don't know what it means to live as God intended them to live? Where can we point them? Where can we find answers ourselves? The best place to start is the Scriptures. And it just so happens that at the beginning of the New Testament we meet the model of manhood—Joseph of Nazareth. Matthew presents him to us in a moment of crisis:

> This is how the birth of Jesus Christ came about: His mother Mary was pledged to be married to Joseph, but before they came together, she was found to be with child through the Holy Spirit. Because Joseph her husband was a righteous man and did not want to expose her to public disgrace, he had in mind to divorce her quietly.
>
> But after he had considered this, an angel of the Lord appeared to him in a dream and said, "Joseph son of David, do not be afraid to take Mary home as your wife, because what is conceived in her is from the Holy Spirit. She will give birth to a son, and you are to give him the name Jesus, because he will save his people from their sins." All this took place to fulfill what the Lord had said

> through the prophet: "The virgin will be with child and will give birth to a son, and they will call him Immanuel"—which means, "God with us." When Joseph woke up, he did what the angel of the Lord had commanded him and took Mary home as his wife. But he had no union with her until she gave birth to a son. And he gave him the name Jesus. (Matt. 1:18–25, ESV)

This passage tells me four things about Joseph. First, he was a man of integrity. In spite of the temptations that any healthy young man faces, his relations with his betrothed and with every other woman were entirely pure. Second, he was willing to sacrifice his reputation for the sake of Mary's. He was selfless, caring more about Mary than himself. Third, he was willing to do the hard thing. He could have taken a much easier and more convenient road and quietly divorced her. Finally, it tells me that Joseph was obedient to the Lord's command. He had a free will and could have dismissed the message of the dream. But his prompt obedience is a model of what makes a real man and a great husband.

HOW MARRIAGE CHANGES MEN AND HOW MARRIAGE CHANGED ME

Change rarely comes easy for any of us. We tend to prefer the predictable and the status quo. Even when we know we should make some changes in our life, we can be reluctant to make them. It's like the story of the young man who stopped by a hardware store on a Saturday morning. A black Labrador was lying on the old wooden floor by the cash register emitting a low groaning noise. "I think your dog is in pain," said the customer. "Do you know what's wrong with him?"

The clerk replied, "He is in pain. He's lying on a nail."

"Why doesn't he get up?" the customer asked.

"Because it's not hurting bad enough," shrugged the clerk.

Many of us know that we *need* to change some of our bad and unhealthy habits. We might even *want* to change. But are we willing to make the effort to do so?

When Jean and I were married thirty years ago, I was twenty-five years of age. By then, I had encountered more than my share of hardships, including the loss of both my parents. I knew what it meant to be alone, to have no one to worry about me, let alone to love me. As a ten-year-old, I had been accused of trying to kill my foster father. I had been ridiculed, dismissed, and shunned. In the first quarter-century of my life, I had seen men die, one in my arms and two others in a horrific plane crash outside my apartment window. I had been exposed to every vice and temptation imaginable. When my schooling took me to Japan, I began to appreciate the size and diversity of the world, and life no longer revolved around a small desert town in Southern California. I had experienced a lot in the few years I had under my belt, but it seems like nothing compared with what I've seen in three decades of marriage.

Marriage has changed me in profound and mysterious ways. I've been confronted with the reality of my own sinfulness and selfishness and yet overwhelmed by the reality of God's lavish grace. I've been reminded how impatient I am and how patient the Lord and Jean are with me. I've learned the power of a sincere and quick apology and the foolishness of excuses. Taking pride in being right is always wrong.

Over the past three decades, I've come to appreciate the significance of tears. I've learned to see through the hollow smiles that often hide sorrow and grief. The difficulty of marriage has driven me to frustration and to my knees in prayer. In the smile of my wife, I've seen the face of God—tender, gentle, and filled with unconditional love. In the two children she has borne, I see His assurance that He has a plan for tomorrow, even if tomorrow's plan remains a mystery to me.

Marriage has taught me that it's the little things that matter. It's the note on the mirror, the wink on your way out the door. It's flowers for no real reason, sitting by the fire together on a cold night, or walking hand in hand along the shore as the sun slips beyond the horizon. It's a text or a call to simply check in, it's remembering what she thinks you'll forget. It's introducing her to all your friends and talking her up in meetings or on the third tee with your golfing buddies. It's surprising her, delighting in her...it's loving her like nobody else in the world ever has or ever will.

Marriage has reminded me of the brevity of life. It's taught me that yesterday is history, tomorrow is mystery, but today—today is the main event! It's okay to take chances—just don't take your time with your wife or your family for granted. I want to urge you to stand up, step up, and embrace your role as a man in today's confused society. It's never too late to start. Be the kind of man that your wife and children so desperately need and desire. Being this kind of man is not just about displaying your physical power. It's about serving your loved ones and neighbors and always doing what is right, regardless of the consequences. Remember David's dying charge to his son Solomon: "Be strong, and show yourself a man, and keep the charge of the Lord your God, walking in his ways and keeping his statutes, his commandments, his rules and his testimonies,...that you may prosper in all that you do and wherever you turn" (1 Kings 2:1–3, ESV).

CHAPTER FIVE

Vive la Différence!

Women transform male lust into love; channel male wanderlust into jobs, homes, and families; link men to specific children; rear children into citizens; change hunters into fathers; divert male will to power into a drive to create. Women conceive the future that men tend to flee.[1]

—George Gilder

The contingent sent by the Virginia Company of London in 1607 to settle Jamestown consisted of two hundred rugged individuals. Some came to convert the Indians to Christianity. Others were pursuing more worldly goals, such as the New World's fabled gold and a northwest passage to the Orient. But one thing was missing from that first group of settlers—women. The historian Alf J. Mapp Jr. observes that "it was thought that women had no place in the grim and often grisly business of subduing a continent."[2] Yet without women, the success of the British venture in Virginia was limited. Why?

Gail Collins notes that without women present, the men weren't very productive, suggesting that they basically "goofed off" most of the time.[3] Without wives and families, they had no motivation to produce more than what they needed to get by. When the women began arriving, in 1608, they were "marooned in what must have seemed like a long, rowdy fraternity party, minus food."[4] A settler who came in 1611 found the men engaged in "their daily and usual workes, bowling in the streets."[5] But soon the women became wives, the apathy gave way to industry, and the colony was flourishing within a few decades.

What happened? I think it's pretty obvious. Marriage gave this ragtag group of men a purpose. Women, especially *wives*, were the key ingredient. As Sir Edwin Sandys, the treasurer of the Virginia Company, wrote, "The plantation can never flourish till families be planted and the respect of wives and children fix the people on the soil."[6] In 1619, the company ordered that "a fit hundredth might be sent of women, maids young and uncorrupt, to make wives to the inhabitants and by that means to make the men there more settled and less movable. . . ."[7] Ninety such women arrived in May 1622, and later accounts record that "57 young maids have been sent to make wives for the planters, divers of which were well married before the coming away of the ships."[8]

Today, some might object that these women were instrumentalized for economic gain. But the story of Jamestown teaches us that no society can thrive without women—specifically, women who are partners in strong and healthy marriages.

THE BIBLE AND WOMEN

It has become common to criticize the Bible, and thus Christianity, as misogynistic, but this indictment ignores what the Scriptures actually have to say about women. For example, in the very first chapter of Genesis, we're told that both male and female were created "in the image of God" (1:27). Deborah, the wife of Lappidoth, was given the authority to judge Israel (Judg. 4:4). And we're all familiar with the thirty-first chapter of Proverbs, Solomon's moving tribute to the "virtuous woman," who is "far more precious than jewels": "She opens her mouth with wisdom, and the teaching of kindness is on her tongue. She looks well to the ways of her household, and does not eat the bread of idleness. Her children rise up and call her blessed; her husband also, and he praises her...." (Prov. 31:26–28, ESV).

In the New Testament, it is the women who are closest to the central mysteries of salvation. Luke's Gospel opens with Elizabeth and her kinswoman the Virgin Mary, to whom God grants a deeper understanding of the miracle of the Incarnation than their holy but occasionally befuddled husbands enjoy. And "standing by the cross of Jesus," when all his disciples but John had fled, "were his mother, and his mother's sister, Mary the wife of Clopas, and Mary Magdalene" (John 19:25, ESV). The same Mary Magdalene was the first to see the risen Christ and the first herald of the Resurrection (John 20:1–18).

The book of Acts frequently depicts women playing critical roles in the early Church. "A disciple named Tabitha" was so valued that Peter himself, summoned at her death, raised her from the dead (9:36–41). The merchant Lydia was one of the first to respond to Paul's preaching on the continent of Europe, bringing her entire household to the faith (16:14–15), and "a woman named Damaris" was among the few Athenians converted by the apostle (17:34).

In his epistles, Paul acknowledges numerous women who have "worked hard in the Lord" with him (Rom. 16:12, ESV), providing indispensable support for his ministry. Surely he had in mind women like the heroic Priscilla, the wife of Aquila, when he enjoined husbands to love their wives "just as Christ also loved the church" (Eph. 5:25, NASB). In short, the Bible isn't just pro-women and pro-marriage; it provides the truest and most complete model of femininity.

Throughout history, life for women has been considerably bleaker in cultures not informed by biblical faith, as John MacArthur, a pastor and frequent guest on the Focus on the Family radio broadcast, explains with bracing clarity:

> I contend that women are used and abused more today than at any time in history. Pornography turns women into objects and victims of dirty, cowardly Peeping Toms who leer at them with greedy eyes. Throughout the world, women are traded like animals for sexual slavery. In more "civilized" places, men routinely use women for no-consequence, no-commitment sex only to leave them pregnant, without care and support. Abortion rights groups aid and abet male selfishness and irresponsibility, and they "free" women to murder their unborn children. Women are left alone, emotionally scarred, financially destitute, and experientially guilty, ashamed, and abandoned. Where's the freedom, dignity, and honor in that?
>
> Modern technological advances have enabled the culture to mainstream the degradation of women like never before; but ancient cultures were no better. Women in pagan societies during biblical times were often treated with little more dignity than animals. Some of the best-known Greek philosophers—considered the brightest minds of their era—taught that women are inferior creatures by nature. Even in the Roman Empire (perhaps the very pinnacle of pre-Christian civilization) women were usually regarded as mere chattel—personal possessions of their husbands or fathers, with hardly any better standing than household slaves. That was vastly different from the Hebrew (and biblical) concepts of marriage as a joint inheritance, and parenthood as a partnership where both father

> and mother are to be revered and obeyed by the children (Leviticus 19:3).[9]

MacArthur's blunt assessment of pagan culture (both ancient and modern) might strike some as harsh, but I'm afraid he's right. While women today have unprecedented opportunities, they are at the same time confronted with a culture so corrosive that moms and dads of teenage and twenty-something daughters lose sleep at night.

THE GENDER WARS

Today, the topic of masculine and feminine roles has become almost "too hot to handle," so I want to make it clear that I'm not making a case for a return to *Leave It to Beaver* days, however enticing and attractive that scenario might seem to some of us. That world had its own problems—racism and segregation, obviously, and women's opportunities were much more limited than they are today. In any case, stay-at-home mothering, which can be an amazing blessing, is a product of prosperity. Not every family is in a position to have a mother work full-time in the home. In fact, stay-at-home mothering, which we often call "traditional," is still a relatively new development. Before the industrial revolution, families farmed together or ran small businesses. The father didn't leave the home, he worked it! The mother also assisted in the family enterprise in addition to raising the children.

The minute you broach the topic of sex roles, many people assume you're talking about how responsibilities are divided up in families. But the issue is much larger than who brings home the bacon and who fries it in the pan. Nevertheless, "traditional" distinctions between men and women and their respective roles are not only essential to a proper understanding of God's design for human life but crucial to the survival of the family and of society as a whole.

Some (perhaps many) aspects of traditional male and female roles are merely human conventions, matters that God leaves to our prudential discretion. But there are limits to that discretion. Radical feminists and their allies have dashed headlong over the cliff of common sense, a cause for the deepest concern.

LOOKING AT SEX ROLES FROM GOD'S POINT OF VIEW

It's been said that God reveals His truth by way of two books—the book of Scripture and the book of nature—which, properly understood, complement one another. Do these two books support our perspectives on masculinity and femininity? I think so. Sometimes Scripture expresses the fundamental distinctions between the sexes so simply that it's easy to miss. Consider Christ's affirmation that "from the beginning, He made them male and female" (Matt. 19:4; Gen. 1:27). From this statement flow a multitude of implications—the inescapable "givens" of sexuality itself.

We start with the attraction between the sexes and its consummation in sexual intercourse. The conception and pregnancy, childbearing and nursing that follow are biologically assigned to the female, while the male is free to look after other necessities of life and to support and protect the female and her offspring. It is natural, then, that certain roles should become associated with the one or the other sex. Because of human artifice and technological innovation, modern societies have been able, to some extent, to avoid (and thus disparage) the pattern of nature. Perhaps this is one of the ways in which civilization and technology have dehumanized us more than we suspect.

If you remove the sediment of mere convention, a bedrock of authentic functional distinctions between the sexes remains. That bedrock, I believe, is tampered with only at great risk to the family, to society, and to our humanity itself.

ROLES WITHIN MARRIAGE

A discussion of male and female roles within marriage always elicits a robust response, whether at a party or in a Sunday school classroom. While I fully affirm the equality of husband and wife in the sight of God, I do not believe in the sameness of their offices or functions. The Bible clearly distinguishes between male and female roles within the marital bond without suggesting that one partner is superior to the other. Instead, functioning together in a complementary relationship of mutual submission, the Christian husband and wife become, as the letter to the Ephesians teaches, a reflection of the love that exists between Christ and His Church.

Let's go a little deeper. The scriptural pathway here is narrow, and it is easy to fall into error on either side. The first error is male domination and female suppression. Yes, the Bible makes it clear that a man should bear the responsibility for leadership in the home, but his wife submits to him only as a leader (Eph. 5:22), not as a tyrant or superior being. The husband's leadership does not rob his wife of her personhood, nor does he have the right to run roughshod over her opinions and feelings. He is to love and cherish her—to *die* for her if necessary—even as Christ loved the Church (Eph. 5:25). He is to include her in important decisions, considering her views carefully and respectfully. What smart husband does not do that? In the end, though, the prerogative—and responsibility—of deciding is allotted to him alone, obliging him to become more sensitive and more considerate, since he must ultimately answer to God for his choices and for the way he treats his wife.

The second error we must avoid is equally dangerous. Given the "male bashing" in media and entertainment, it is easy to forget about the importance of masculine leadership altogether. In my opinion, the breakdown of many families today is due in large part to the failure of men to assume their God-given responsibilities. If, trying to avoid male domination, we swing to the other extreme and strip husbands of their authority, we will be disregarding God's plan for marriage and the family and ultimately courting social disaster.

CHAPTER SIX

Why Children Need Both a Mother and a Father

[T]he principal social objective of American national government at every level... [should be] to see that children are born to intact families and that they remain so and that this become an object of the churches, of the society at large.[1]

—Senator Daniel Patrick Moynihan

The memory is vivid. And painful. I was a sophomore, and nothing else excited me as much as a Friday night playing football under the lights. But on this particular autumn evening, I had a pit in my stomach. That's because it was "Dad Night" at Yucca Valley High School. I would rather have been almost anyplace else on earth. The stands were packed with families—mothers and fathers, brothers and sisters, grandparents. Our team jogged out onto the field and looked up to the announcer's booth as the ceremonies got under way. One by one, the names of my teammates' fathers were called. Each dad would run out onto the field, hug or high-five his son, and take his place proudly by his side. When my name was called, my father didn't run onto the field. "Jim Daly's father is not present tonight," came the booming announcement. I felt as though everyone in the Yucca Valley School District heard it. I hung my head and silently sighed, a wave of private sorrow sweeping over me.

Those few seconds almost forty years ago—"Jim Daly's father is not present"—summed up all the pain of my childhood. By high school, my father's absence was simply a fact of life, but it hadn't become any easier. It never does. One of the great misconceptions about broken families is the supposed resiliency of the kids. I hear it all the time. "Oh, kids are tough," they say. "They'll bounce back. They'll be okay."

But sadly, just believing something doesn't necessarily make it so.

It's tough to go through life with a father or mother who's either physically or emotionally absent. But don't take my word for it; just look at the statistics. Since the vast majority of single-parent homes are led by women, here's a snapshot of how things go awry when a dad's not at home:

- 71 percent of all high school dropouts come from fatherless homes.
- 85 percent of all youth in prison come from fatherless homes.
- 90 percent of all homeless and runaway children come from fatherless homes.[2]

Does that mean that every child who's missing a parent is destined for disaster? Of course not. But a mountain of social science literature from the past three decades shows that, on average, children do best in every important measure of health and well-being when they are raised by their own (biological) mother and father in a low-conflict married home. This is beyond dispute. We also know a great deal about the measurable educational, psychological, social, and developmental hardships that fatherless children face. More than twenty-four million children in the United States today live apart from their fathers—one out of every three. It's even worse for African American children. Nearly 73 percent of African American boys and girls don't have a dad in the home.[3]

Compounding these challenges is the push to normalize parenting and adoption by same-sex couples. Homosexual advocates contend that all couples are equal and that children fare well in such arrangements. You'll even hear it said that children raised by homosexual couples do *better.* But no credible research has found that a father can be effectively replaced by a mom's lesbian life partner, no matter how loving and caring she might be. The studies that purport to show otherwise are deficient on a number of levels. For one thing, they have relied on small samples of subjects who knew they were participating in the research and self-reported the well-being of their children. If persons interested in a particular result can directly affect the study's data, the study doesn't tell you much.

Social scientists with varying viewpoints on homosexuality concur that it is still too early to draw meaningful conclusions about the effects of homosexual parenting on children. The few unbiased studies point to a number of disadvantages. The fact of the matter is that a father plays a role in his children's lives that no one else can fill. And so does a mother.

A diverse collection of family scholars at the Universities of Texas, Virginia, Minnesota, Chicago, Maryland, and Washington, at the University of California at Berkeley, and at Rutgers University recently reported on the multiple benefits for children of living with their own, married parents.[4] In general, within this family structure, children

- live longer, healthier lives both physically and mentally,
- do better in school,
- are more likely to attend and complete college,

- are less likely to live in poverty,
- are less likely to get in trouble with the law,
- are less likely to drink or use drugs,
- are less likely to be violent or sexually active,
- are less likely to be victims of sexual or physical violence, and
- are more likely to have successful marriages when they are older.

SCIENCE ONCE AGAIN AFFIRMS THE SCRIPTURES

My faith doesn't need to be confirmed by anything outside the Scriptures, but it's gratifying when scientific research affirms the word of God, as it does—abundantly—on the subject of marriage and the family. At the same time, isn't the question of whether a child needs both a mother and a father simply a matter of common sense?

On this issue, however, many good and intelligent people seem to ignore common sense. Perhaps you have friends or neighbors who see nothing wrong with the evolving definition of family. Even if they did, they would probably be reluctant to challenge the politically correct line that a family of any configuration will get the job done. Or maybe your own grown son or daughter believes the traditional understanding of parenting is hopelessly old-fashioned. If that's the case, I'd like to get very practical here and provide you with some reasons why children need both a mother and a father. I'm fortunate to have as a colleague at Focus on the Family Glenn Stanton, one of the foremost scholars of the family, who has provided this summary of the enormous volume of research in this field.

1. Mothers and fathers parent differently

Are you surprised? Aren't you different from your spouse? This difference is crucially important for children. The cooperation of male and female in marriage blends their differences to provide a child with good things that same-sex caregivers cannot. I see this in my own marriage. Jean is naturally nurturing and helps the boys get organized. I'm more spontaneous and encourage Trent and Troy to dream big and take smart risks. Years ago, the famed German psychologist Erik Erickson explained that father love and mother love are qualitatively different. Fathers "love more dangerously," he wrote, because their love is more "expectant, more instrumental" than a mother's love.[5] In recent years, scores of other social scientists have confirmed what Erickson found decades ago.

2. Mothers and fathers play differently

I can't remember Jean's ever wrestling with Trent or Troy, but for me it's a nightly ritual. A recent study reveals that 70 percent of father-infant games are physical and action-oriented while only 4 percent of mother-infant play is characterized as such. In play, mothers stress equity and security, while fathers encourage independence and competition. When's the last time a five-year-old girl wore out the knees of her jeans? None of Trent's jeans have ever been in good enough shape to pass down to Troy. According to the fathering expert John Snarey, children who roughhouse with their fathers learn that biting, kicking, and other forms of physical violence are not acceptable. They learn self-control by being told when "enough is enough" and when to "settle down." Girls and boys both learn a healthy balance between timidity and aggression. Children need mom's softness as well as dad's roughhousing. Both provide security and confidence in their own ways by communicating love and physical intimacy.

3. Mothers and fathers communicate differently

When the boys were old enough to begin daily family devotions, Jean preferred a scheduled devotional time at home, while I preferred leading devotions in the car on the drive to school. Neither of us is right or wrong. It's just a matter of style. Again it shouldn't come as a shock that mothers and fathers speak differently to children. Mothers simplify their words and speak on the child's level. Men are not as inclined to modify their language for the child. Both styles help a child's communication skills develop. Take away one and the child is poorer for it.

4. Mothers and fathers discipline differently

I admit there are times when my boys manage to push all of my buttons until I bark. In those emotionally charged moments, Trent and Troy witness their otherwise loving, huggable, and tender daddy undergo a metamorphosis much like Dr. Banner's in *The Incredible Hulk*. Don't get me wrong—Jean can blow her stack too, but disciplining children isn't about our tempers. It's about how we're wired to correct bad behavior and shape our kids' actions.

The psychologist Carol Gilligan suggests that fathers tend to stress justice, fairness, and duty (based on rules), while mothers stress sympathy, care, and help (based on relationships).[6] Fathers tend to enforce rules systematically and sternly, teaching children objectivity and the consequences of right and wrong. Mothers tend toward grace and sympathy in the midst of disobedience, providing a sense of hopefulness. Again, either approach by itself is not sufficient, but together they produce a healthy balance. I know these stereotypes don't apply to every family. In fact, they don't apply to ours. When it comes to discipline, Jean stresses the rules. After all, without them there's chaos! I, on the other hand, am more lenient and nurturing. We're a good balance for one another.

5. Fathers and mothers prepare children for life differently

As Glenn Stanton has observed, "Dads tend to see their child in relation to the rest of the world. Mothers tend to see the rest of the world in relation to their child."[7] This is a very good thing. To use a sporting metaphor, I think fathers are the coaches on the sidelines or at the chalkboard sketching out the plays; mothers are the trainers and chaplains, nurturing and listening. That doesn't mean that fathers don't nurture and mothers don't coach, but it does mean that the parent of each sex models a particular strength.

6. Fathers provide a look at the world of men; mothers at the world of women

Once again, this one is something of a no-brainer, but it's an important point to make. There's a psychological difference between the sexes. Yes, there are overstated stereotypes—men like sports and women like to shop. We all know people who deviate from the norm or are a mixture of both. But stereotypes can be based on well-established facts and trends. In addition, we now know that there are important physiological differences between the sexes, including the following:

- "As a rule, a male brain is about 10 percent heavier than a female brain, reflecting general difference in body size."[8]
- Women's brains show "significantly stronger patterns of interconnectivity across brain regions—including *across* the hemispheres."[9]
- Men's brains show "significantly greater connectivity *within* local brain regions."[10]
- "Women tend to do better on tests measuring sensitivity to odors." A woman's sense of smell is also linked to "her monthly production of hormones, reaching a peak at ovulation."[11]
- "Although some women are stronger than some men, the average man's heavier bones, bulkier muscles, broader shoulders and larger heart and lungs make him physically stronger than the average woman."[12]
- On average, the areas of the brain involving language and fine-motor skills mature earlier in girls, while the parts of the brain involved in targeting and spatial memory mature earlier in boys.[13]
- During adolescence in girls, "a larger fraction of the brain activity associated with negative emotion moves

up to the cerebral cortex.... So, the seventeen-year-old is able to explain why she is feeling sad in great detail and without much difficulty (if she wants to). But that change occurs *only in girls*. In boys, the locus of brain activity associated with negative emotion remains stuck in the amygdala."[14]

- "Studies in the United States and around the world universally find that boys are more likely to engage in physically risky activities."[15]

The anthropologist Suzanne Frayser stresses the critical importance of fathers and mothers for their sons and daughters. "The boy can look at his father and see what he should do to be a male; he can look at his mother and see what he should not do to be a male."[16] She continues, "The importance of contrasts in gender roles and specification of gender identity may be clues to the psychological importance of sexual differentiation in all societies."[17]

7. Fathers and mothers teach respect for the opposite sex

A married father is substantially less likely to abuse the woman and children with whom he lives than a man in any other category. This means that boys and girls with fathers generally learn, by observation, how men should treat women. Speaking personally, a substantial portion of the time I spend with my sons is devoted to the topic of manners and respect. I regularly remind them that a real man never hurts a woman. Sure, mothers can and do teach this truth, but showing is almost always more powerful than simply telling. Studies confirm the value of fathers when it comes to teaching the love and respect of women. The *American Journal of Sociology* reports, "Societies with father-present patterns of child socialization produce men who are less inclined to exclude women from public activities than their counterparts in father-absent societies."[18]

As Glenn Stanton concludes, "To be concerned with proper child development is to be concerned about making sure that children have daily access to the different and complementary ways mothers and fathers parent. Children greatly benefit from the presence of both a mother and a father. Without it, boys and girls will be at greater risk for gender confusion, abuse, and exploitation from other men. They are less likely to have a healthy respect for both women and men as they grow into adulthood."[19]

THE FATHER NEED

In a recent poll by the National Center for Fathering, 92 percent of respondents said that dads make a "unique contribution" to the lives of their children, and seven out of ten see absentee dads as the biggest family or social problem facing the United States.[20] Research backs up such a belief. About 44 percent of children in mother-only households live in poverty, according to a 2011 U.S. Census study, compared with 12 percent of children living in intact homes.[21] These kids are more likely to have trouble with alcohol or drugs, to cause trouble in school, and to have run-ins with the law.

The statistics for fatherless girls are no better. They too struggle as kids and into adulthood. Moreover, females raised without fathers are four times more likely to engage in sexual intercourse at an early age and more than twice as likely to get pregnant early.[22]

If you look at virtually *any* measure of the mental and emotional health of children and how they make the transition into adulthood, kids with involved dads simply do better.

Dr. Bill Maier, a family psychologist and the host of a nationally broadcast radio show, saw the devastating effects of fatherlessness firsthand during the years he worked at a community mental-health clinic in Long Beach, California. He recalls:

> Most of the children with whom I worked were low-income kids from single-parent homes. Many of these boys and girls had never met their fathers. Others had dads who were living on the street, involved in gangs, in prison, or dead. The young boys, in particular, had an incredible hunger for male attention and affirmation. They cherished the one hour each week that I met with them for their individual counseling session. When I visited them at their public school, their eyes would light up and they would excitedly tell their friends, "That's my *counselor*—he's here to see *me*!" Often, their classmates (who were also fatherless) would gather around and ask, "Can you be my counselor, too?" My heart broke for these children, who were aching for a man simply to talk to them and take an interest in their lives. The psychiatrist Kyle Pruett at Yale University calls this longing "fatherneed," and it perfectly describes what millions of boys and girls in the United States experience every day of their lives.

Indeed, this "fatherneed" is clearly what drives many of America's twenty-four million fatherless kids to turn to sex, alcohol, crime, and other dangerous and deadly behaviors. It is only by the grace of God that I was not swallowed up by these destructive forces. When I look back at my childhood, I shudder at some of the memories. There was the time a man died right outside my bedroom window in Compton, California, a victim of gang violence. How did I avoid gang life and all the horrors that accompany it? So many hours of my childhood were spent alone when other friends of mine were playing ball, tinkering in the garage, or camping with their fathers. A kind bus driver once saved me from what was likely the advances of a pedophile. I cannot explain why I was spared such evils while others my own age fell prey, but make no mistake, the fact that I am currently president of a family ministry, rather than in prison, does not mean that I was not damaged by my father's behavior. Our chaotic relationship so wounded my spirit that it is difficult to talk about even today. Nevertheless, I learned at an early age that "all things work together for good for those who love God, who are called according to his purpose" (Rom. 8:28, NET.)

I also learned that ours is a God who can be trusted. Even at this very moment, His prevenient grace is preparing the way and days ahead.

CHAPTER SEVEN

In Good Times and in Bad

The difficulty with marriage is that we fall in love with a personality, but must live with a character.

—Peter de Vries

I want you to meet Doug Groothuis, a professor of philosophy at Denver Seminary and a leading Christian apologist. In late 2015, Doug surprised many people with an article in *Christianity Today* revealing the serious problems that he and his wife, Becky, had faced in their thirty-year marriage:

> A gifted writer and editor, Becky had been bedeviled by a bevy of chronic illnesses, each year worse than the year before. None were fatal. All were miserable. They handed down not a death sentence, but a life sentence. It was ailment upon ailment without respite. We lamented as we sought relief.

> The losses compounded and gathered into a pattern of a life absent of common enjoyments such as vacations, sufficient sleep, church attendance, days and even hours free from pain, serendipitous activities, and more. In their place came doctors' visits, medical tests, prescriptions, expensive supplements, counseling, prayer sessions, experiments with unorthodox medical practitioners, and more. Our searches for respite did not do much good. I often thought of Freud's statement that at its best, psychoanalysis could bring "an acceptable level of misery." That was about all we had.
>
> The strain upon our marriage was heavy, sometimes crushing. But we took our vows to each other and before God seriously, and we soldiered on. I could find the solid ground of meaning in my writing and teaching. But for Becky, the sicker she became, the more these islands of meaning sank beneath her.[1]

Doug goes on to share details of their difficult, decades-long journey, an odyssey that continues to this day. Becky has now been diagnosed with dementia, and Doug's sorrow is palpable. "Besides Becky," he writes, "I have almost no living relations. Because of her health, we have no children. I am an only child. My parents are dead. My relatives are distant geographically and not that close emotionally."[2] He concludes by turning to the book of Ecclesiastes and to the Psalms, which "recognize and ratify my anger, confusion, and fatigue, while placing them in the grand story of Scripture and before the presence of God. Still, I lament before God and man, trying to find a sure footing where I will not sink into self-pity and where I can smelt meaning out of misery—a footing from which I can offer up to God and to the world a hope worth hoping, because there is a God worth knowing."[3]

The circumstances that Doug and Becky Groothuis find themselves in today are not what they envisioned on the morning of their wedding. They had hopes and dreams, and no one thought of a time when "sorrows like sea billows roll." But even if you never face hardships like those the Groothuises have endured, marriage is difficult because it's a union of sinners.

MARITAL DIFFICULTY IS NO LAUGHING MATTER

The comedian Jeff Allen and his wife, Tami, once joined me in the radio studio to share the challenges they've experienced in their marriage. Years earlier, their marriage was all but dead. It was past acrimony and fighting. After years of her husband's alcoholism and fits of rage, Tami always had her back to Jeff. One night, he tried to talk to her in bed, but she refused to turn around. "No—please," she said.

"What's the problem?" he asked.

"I...I can't, Jeff."

"You can't look at me?" he sputtered.

"No," Tami answered.

In ten years, they had gone from "I do" to "I can't look at you." How does that happen?

Jeff explained that his drinking and temper were hurting the family. He hit bottom when he beat his six-month-old son, who was crying only because he was hungry. "Nothing as a man could have shamed me more than that," Jeff remembers.

A friend had given Jeff a subscription to a Bible study on tape, and for a year the cassettes had accumulated in a junk drawer. By this point, Tami and the kids were leaving Jeff to spend the summer with her parents. She needed to get away from him. He wasn't the man she had married. Before she left, Tami threw the Bible study tapes on the floor and said, "You either listen to these things or I'm throwing them out." Jeff did listen to those tapes. And that's what God used to start this couple on the long, seemingly impossible road to reconciliation.

Today, Jeff and Tami Allen can rejoice that God has carried out a miracle in their marriage. "God has restored all.... He's restored everything," says Jeff.

Just as God breathed new life into the dry bones so that they "lived and stood on their feet," He can resuscitate a marriage that's as good as dead. We've seen Him do it time and time again here at Focus on the Family. In fact, if you're in a challenging marriage or know someone who's ready to sign the divorce papers, I want to make sure you're aware of Focus on the Family's Hope Restored marriage intensives, a ministry in Branson, Missouri, that helps marriages in crisis. To qualify for our program, couples must answer "yes" to one simple but profound question: If God were to work a miracle in your marriage, would you accept it?

The retreat center carries out highly successful marriage intensives led by licensed marriage therapists. It's like an emergency room for couples in crisis. Couples stay for multiple-day sessions so they can take full advantage of the most effective treatment model known to the professional counseling world. The results are extraordinary. Since 2003, more than three thousand couples have stayed at the Branson retreat center. Follow-up research indicates that more than 84 percent of them are still married two years later!

CHRISTIANS STRUGGLE, BUT THEY DON'T HAVE TO STRUGGLE ALONE

It can be tempting to think that our faith will—or at least should—inoculate us from marital strife. After all, Christian history is full of heartwarming stories of great marriages—Martin

Luther's loving union to Katharina von Bora, Sarah Pierpont's incredible support of Jonathan Edwards and their eleven children, Charles Spurgeon and his beloved "wifey" Susannah, and, more recently, Billy and Ruth Graham. (Incidentally, Ruth was once asked if in all her years married to Billy, she had ever thought of divorce. She replied humorously, "No, not divorce. But I did think of murder a few times."[4]) But while marriages may be "conceived" in Heaven, they have to be lived out on earth, with all its trials and tribulations. John Wesley, the founder of the Methodist movement, and the great revivalist George Whitefield struggled mightily in their own marriages, having neglected their wives in favor of preaching and spreading the Gospel. In recent years we have witnessed the divorces of high-profile Christian leaders like Dr. Charles Stanley, the founder of In Touch Ministries.[5] Three of Billy and Ruth Graham's five children have divorced, as has their grandson Tullian Tchividjian.[6]

The people God uses for great and mighty works are as capable as any of us of making a mess of their marriages. Indeed, it has happened in the radio ministry at Focus on the Family. When it has, critics have accused the men involved and our ministry of hypocrisy. Is that a fair charge? It would be difficult for me to disagree. That's why I so often lament the Christian divorce rate. Yes, those who take their faith seriously have a lower divorce rate than nominal believers and the unchurched, but it's still too high. Our actions must be consistent with our faith.

All of us are vulnerable to marital challenges. Marriage is tough. Let me tell you a story about a friend of mine who nearly got divorced, Dr. Greg Smalley, the vice president of marriage ministries at Focus on the Family and the son of the popular author and speaker Dr. Gary Smalley. Not only is he a marriage expert, he also has a great sense of humor. Greg and his wife, Erin, have been married for twenty-one years and have four children. But would it surprise you to learn that after the first two years the Smalleys' marriage was in dire straits? It's true.

I want to share the story—and what ultimately saved their marriage. Greg and Erin will tell you they weren't very good at managing the conflicts and pressures that beset most young couples in graduate school. That's embarrassing if you're the son of a famous expert on marriage and family and a candidate for a master's degree in counseling. So Greg and Erin, in shame and confusion, swept their marital problems under the rug. Fortunately, they weren't able to fool *everyone*. Greg's supervisor, Dr. Gary Oliver, sensed that something was wrong. And Dr. Oliver's wife, Carrie, a fellow student of Greg's and a special friend to Erin, shared her husband's misgivings.

Unfortunately, there wasn't much the Olivers could do—not while Greg and Erin chose to keep up their painful masquerade. Things might have gone on this way for a long time if it weren't for a fateful phone call. Erin happened to be out running errands when Greg, tired and frazzled at the end of a hectic day, picked up the receiver and heard Carrie's voice on the other end of the line.

"Sorry," he said dully when she asked to speak to his wife. "Erin's gone."

"*Gone*?" responded Carrie. "Oh, dear! Gary and I were afraid it would come to this!"

Greg had only meant that Erin was gone for a bit, but Carrie's reaction revealed something frightening: *The cat's out of the bag*! Greg didn't know whether to cry or breathe a sigh of relief.

"Greg," said the voice after a long pause, "I have a feeling we need to talk. Would you and Erin like to come over for a while?"

To make a long story short, that's exactly what they did. When Erin got home, the two of them went straight to the Olivers' home, where they spent the evening in prayer, discussion, confession, and honest reflection. Greg remembers it as a turning point in their marriage. It was more than just a lesson in understanding his wife at a deeper level: it was the beginning of a long-term *relationship* with an older, wiser, more experienced couple—a communal connection that would be a source of indispensable guidance, solace, encouragement, and reassurance for the next fifteen years.

It was a relational revolution, and at Focus on the Family we're working with Drs. Les and Leslie Parrott to provide other couples with the same kind of help the Olivers extended to the Smalleys. We call the initiative Focus Marriage Mentors. Mentor couples don't have to have a perfect relationship, and they don't have to have been married for decades. They don't even have to have an answer to every question. All they need is to be one step ahead of another couple and willing to share how God has gotten them through the challenges of married life. Are you interested in lending a hand? Maybe you and your spouse overcame cultural differences. Perhaps you're part of a blended family and together you weathered the challenges of bringing together two sets of children. It might be that you still remember how tough it was to maintain your relationship through multiple military deployments. Maybe you and your spouse have survived sleepless nights with small children and can now offer a word of encouragement to weary moms and dads. Perhaps you've ridden the roller coaster of adoption and feel led to walk alongside another couple as they journey to build their family. Whatever it is, you and your spouse have a story of God's faithfulness in your lives and marriage. He carried you through something, and you learned some hard lessons along the way.

The Apostle Paul wrote repeatedly of enduring adversity. Writing to the church at Corinth, he suggested that one reason God helps us through our own troubles is "so that we may be able to comfort those who are in any affliction, with the comfort with which we ourselves are comforted by God" (2 Cor. 1:4, ESV). In other words, you've got to "pay it forward." And if you do so with Focus Marriage Mentors, you're joining more than 250,000 couples who are working to turn the tide for marriage. You'll discover what they've already learned—that if you invest in another's marriage, you receive a tenfold blessing in return. Helping someone else's relationship makes your own marriage stronger. You might even say that mentoring is what every marriage needs. If this sounds like something you might like to participate in, please visit our Focus Marriage Mentors website at www.focusonthefamily.com/marriagementors.

THE DIVORCE MYTH

It's been my experience that most people who consider divorce think that being freed from their marital bonds will make them happier. Sociologists, however, have found that the majority of persons in unhappy marriages who were able to avoid divorce reported themselves "very happy" only a few years later.[7] Those who went through with a divorce, on the other hand, were just as unhappy as they were before. In fact, many of them regretted their decision. One of the best long-term studies on divorce found that only 20 percent of couples were happier after a divorce.[8]

The evidence of the destructive effects of divorce is sobering. The life expectancies for divorced men and women are substantially lower than those for married persons (who have the longest life expectancies).[9] The health consequences of divorce are so severe that a Yale researcher concluded that "being divorced and a nonsmoker is slightly less dangerous than smoking a pack a day and staying married."[10] Married persons are more likely to recover from cancer than divorced persons are, suggesting that the emotional trauma of divorce has a long-term effect on physical health.[11] Men and women both suffer a decline in mental health following divorce, but the decline is worse for women.[12] Divorce produces depression, and hostility harms self-acceptance, personal growth, and relations with others.[13]

People often view divorce as a way to end the fighting, but the problems usually don't go away after divorce. In fact, anger and animosity often increase. And the problems aren't solved by a second marriage. So is the moral of the story that simple—never consider divorce? Not necessarily. There are many reasons why couples separate and divorce, and while the Bible makes it clear that God *hates* divorce, it's also true that He provides limited grounds for it. To be sure, ours is a compassionate God; He forgives those who repent and request forgiveness. Christians can rest in the knowledge that He will never forsake those who believe. So if you have been divorced, press forward to help other couples do better. If you've remarried, stay committed.

But let's get back to those couples who, despite their unhappiness, have decided to forgo divorce. What did it take to turn the tide? Was it simply a matter of time? Does time really heal all wounds? As it turns out, the passage of time *is* an important part of resolving conflict. The unhappiness of many couples is due to outside pressures—a job loss, for example, or the demands of young children—and those circumstances eventually change. We also gain perspective when we step back and reevaluate a problem after tempers cool and frustrations cease. But even though many problems resolve themselves if we're patient, we can do more than just wait for our unhappiness to go away. Here are some steps that can help a troubled marriage:

- *Work at it.* How many times have you heard that "poor communication" hurts a marriage? Well, it *does*. Many couples have improved their marriage with small steps, like listening to each other. A husband learns to compliment his wife, for example, and a wife learns to encourage her husband.
- *A change of perspective in one spouse.* Sometimes, one spouse simply decides not to base all of his or her

happiness on the mood of the other spouse. Instead, the spouse might take up a hobby or simply make an attitude adjustment that allows him or her to be more patient and accepting of the other.

- *Credible threat of consequences for bad behavior.* Some marriages are initially unhappy because of one spouse's bad behavior—staying out late, infidelity, or even occasional abuse. The other spouse can take firm action, making it clear that she or he will not tolerate such behavior. Sometimes that's the incentive the misbehaving spouse needs.

As we saw above, divorce frequently leads to increased physical and mental problems. Divorce so often treats the symptom but leaves the cause of the dysfunction unaddressed. It's like a runner repeatedly popping ibuprofen to relieve the chronic pain in his foot. Yes, the pills temporarily reduce the inflammation, but the pain quickly returns because a pill won't cure his plantar fasciitis. Divorce is like an anti-inflammatory. The relief is temporary, and husband and wife transfer their faults and bad habits to another relationship. Without addressing the cause, they're destined to experience the same unhappiness they had in the previous marriage. I can't put it any better than Laura, a woman who regrets her divorce, did in a heartfelt letter:

> The grass is not greener.... I would have done it a different way.... I would not have made the same decision. I would have worked really hard.... I would say [to others facing a decision to divorce], do not evaluate with anger because your anger is an emotion and it will guide you towards a decision that you might not be happy with down the line. I always tell people—and I have plenty of friends who...[are] having problems with their sex lives or this,

> that, and the other, and I say, "I don't care what it is. Figure it out.... And be extremely prayerful about it. Make sure 100% that this is not an emotion-based decision. Because when you base it off of an emotion, you're going to be sorry about the consequences later on." ... Don't make these decisions based on emotion. Try to see past it. Or give yourself some time to step away.... I always steer people not to get a divorce, even though I have had one. And they always say, "Well you did it." Yeah, well, if I had a chance to go back, I probably wouldn't have done it. I tell people, "Look, if he's beating the crap out of you, we've got an issue.... But if it's about anything else, you can work through it." ... People are imperfect. I know he loves me, and I was too stupid and too prideful, even though he did me wrong.

You feel the pain and anguish in Laura's heart. I'm sure you have a loved one or a neighbor who struggles with the regret of a relationship gone bad. Maybe you're the one struggling. Unfulfilled expectations in personal relationships can be terribly difficult to manage. Terri Orbuch, a psychologist at the University of Michigan's Institute for Social Research, has studied the regrets of divorced couples. "Divorced individuals who step back and say, 'This is what I've done wrong and this is what I will change,' have something powerful to teach others," she says.[14] Dr. Orbuch has identified five of the most common regrets of divorced persons. Perhaps they'll help you make a few changes in your own marriage.

1. "I should have made more effort to boost my ex-spouse's mood." Encouraging and affirming your spouse in very simple ways can go a very long way. One study finds that when a husband thinks his wife doesn't express love and affection (not necessarily sex), the couple is twice as likely to divorce. Spontaneous gestures of kindness can go a long way. Buy some flowers, write a letter, look for the humorous side of life.

2. "We should have talked more about money."

Money is a magnifier of problems, but it's also a common source of tension. Don't keep secrets. Establish a family budget and stick to it. There are many helpful resources available. Dave Ramsey, a frequent guest on our radio program, has put together a practical program on finances that every couple can benefit from.

3. "I should have gotten over the past."

Couples who can't forgive past hurts grow bitter and resentful. Talk it out. Write a letter. Talk with a trusted friend.

4. "I should have taken more responsibility for our problems."

Studies suggest that 65 percent of divorced persons blame their ex-spouse for the demise of their marriage. When discussing relationship problems, Dr. Orbuch suggests saying "we," not "you" or "I." For example, you might say, "We are both so tired lately," not "You are so crabby."

5. "I should have shared more of my heart and feelings."

Dr. Orbuch recommends that a couple spend ten minutes every day talking about something other than work, the family and children, the household, the relationship. No problems. No scheduling. No logistics.

BROKEN HEARTS AND BROKEN DREAMS

I know that many of you are enduring the pain of a failing marriage or a divorce that you didn't want. You've done everything you can do to save the marriage, but your spouse or ex-spouse is adamantly opposed to reconciliation. As I've said already, marriage is difficult because it involves two imperfect people, and though you cannot change your spouse, you can change yourself. Changes you make to improve yourself often produce healthy responses in your spouse and might save your marriage.

You can encourage your spouse to communicate better by learning to communicate better yourself. You can show your spouse how to respect you by respecting him or her first. You can teach your spouse to stop complaining with a bitter spirit by breaking your own habit of complaining. Your husband or wife may not be willing to read books, go to seminars, or go to counseling yet, but if you take the first step, your changes may influence him or her.

EVALUATION AND PRACTICAL ADVICE

I'd like to end this chapter by encouraging you to take an honest assessment of your marriage. Every marriage contains its share of challenges. There will be difficult seasons in even the happiest of unions. It might be an overstatement to compare marriage to a rollercoaster, but even a healthy relationship is like a country road, with its twists and turns and occasional dips.

Too many couples—especially Christian couples—expect perfection. If you're going through a rough patch, is it possible that you're making a mountain out of a molehill? As Mark Twain once said of the music of Wagner, it's not as bad as it sounds. Dr. John Gottman, a psychologist and the founder of the Gottman Relationship Institute,[15] has identified six criteria of healthy marriages. I'd like to share them with you. Please review them in light of your own situation:

1. High levels of friendship, respect, affection, and humor

This is defined as liking each other, being each other's best friend, doing things together; showing interest in and respect for the other's thoughts and feelings, avoiding put-downs, supporting each other's goals and aspirations, feeling affection for each other, having fun and laughter together, being number one in each other's eyes.

2. A ratio of 5:1 or better of positive to negative interactions

This means that your relationship averages at least five pleasant, friendly, or loving experiences or periods of time for every hostile word, angry argument, or time spent feeling hurt or resentful. And 5:1 is the minimum!

3. Successful "bids for attention"

When a wife says, "Hey, listen to this!" she is trying to get her husband's attention for a conversation. If the husband keeps on scrolling through Facebook, ignoring her, he's turning away her bid for attention. If he says "Huh?" and lifts his eyes off the sports page for a second or two, he's turning toward her—a good sign. And if he actually listens to what she has to say, that's a real connection! In successful marriages, partners turn toward each other an average of 86 percent of the time. In divorcing couples, the average is 33 percent.

4. Soft starts of disagreements

In successful marriages, disagreements are started softly, without critical, contemptuous remarks about the other person.

5. Husband accepts influence from wife

In successful marriages, husbands accept influence from their wives. If a wife says she's afraid her husband is driving too fast and he responds in irritation, "I know what I'm doing!" this is a shaky marriage. There must be give and take in a relationship. Research shows that women are accustomed to accepting influence from men. So it's crucial that men learn to do the same!

6. Respect for each other's needs, likes, dislikes, and inner life

They ask questions to find out; they listen; they care!

How did you fare? I pray that you sense the urgency in my words when I remind you that next to your relationship with the Lord, the best investment you can make here on earth is the relationship with your spouse. So much hinges on the health of our marriage. Yes, marriage is difficult. But remember, it's not designed to make us happy (though it ultimately will); it's designed to make us holy. As Erich

Fromm, the late German psychologist, wrote, "If love were only a feeling, there would be no basis for the promise to love each other forever." In other words, the wedding vow anticipates the reality of radical difficulty. It's there in the fine print.

If you find yourself in the midst of a difficult marriage, I urge you to seek professional Christian counseling. In fact, I invite you to call our counseling line at Focus on the Family. We will provide an initial consultation and, if needed, provide you with a referral for a counselor in your area. To reach us by phone, please call 1-800-A-Family (232-6459) weekdays 6:00 a.m. to 8:00 p.m. (mountain time). If a counselor is not immediately available, you can leave your contact information, and someone will call you back as soon as possible. This is available at no cost to you.

CHAPTER EIGHT

For the Greater Good

As the family goes, so goes the nation and so goes the whole world in which we live.[1]

—Pope John Paul II

Have you ever wondered what life would be like without the traditional institution of marriage? I'm not talking about what it would be like for you personally, I'm talking about *a world* without biblical marriage. In 1848, John Humphrey Noyes attempted to find out. Expelled from seminary at Yale for his radical and wildly unorthodox beliefs, he settled with a group of followers in the remote village of Oneida, New York, determined to pursue a new and ideal way of life so appealing that the rest of the world would soon follow suit.[2]

Declaring that Christians are no longer capable of sinning—a theological belief known as "perfectionism"—Noyes believed it was necessary to establish the Kingdom of Heaven here on earth.[3] Since

Christ had revealed that there is no marriage in Heaven, marriage should be abolished here as well. In Noyes's community, couples who became exclusively devoted to one another were chastised for being "idolatrous." He replaced monogamous marriage with what he called "complex marriage," in which all the women of the community were wives of all the men and all the men were husbands of all the women. "Free love," however, had its limits. Noyes insisted on monitoring sexual activity in the community, and pregnancies were controlled through a practice known as "coitus reservatus" or "male continence." Childbearing was a community decision. Noyes eventually fled to Canada to avoid prosecution for statutory rape (he often chose sexual partners for himself as young as twelve) and died there in 1886.

Sociologists, surprised that this bizarre community lasted as long as it did, have studied the damage it inflicted on its members. Children were not permitted to live with their biological mother or father but were raised communally. Spencer Klaw relates the heartbreaking testimony of some of the survivors:

> "Darling, do you love me?" asked the mother to her young boy. "I always melted," the boy, then a man, recalled. "My marbles and blocks were forgotten. I would reach up and put my arms about her neck. I remember how tightly she held me and how long, as though she would never let me go." Another female member of the community expressed disgust over the practice of being assigned sexual partners, often at a clip of two or three per week. "I wish," she wrote, "it were more popular than it is for the young to love the old, the handsome to love the less so, the educated the less educated, in short, that love might be truly free, permeating and pervading all hearts."[4]

GOD'S PLAN WORKS BEST

The Oneida Community was just one in a long line of failed social experiments in reimagining marriage and the family, all of which attempted to assume God's authority. We somehow think that when it comes to planning human happiness, we know better than He does. The most recent example has been the successful campaign to redefine marriage in our civil laws to include same-sex unions.

All of these deviations from God's plan are motivated, in one way or another, by selfish desires. We want what we want when we want it, and we ignore or rationalize the effect of our actions on our families and our society. A man will explain away his extramarital affair by lamenting his wife's lack of interest in sex. Likewise, all the arguments in favor of same-sex "marriage" revolve around individual desires. If that means a child will be deprived of a mother or a father, that's just the price of (the adult's) freedom. To quote a popular—and shallow—slogan of today's sexual revolutionaries, "It is what it is."

You know *it is*? I'll tell you. It's sin. St. Augustine of Hippo described man as *incurvatus in se*—"turned inward" and living for himself as opposed to serving others.[5] The root of today's marriage crisis is the same malady that's plagued society from the dawn of time. We want to shape and bend marriage to fit *our own* selfish desires instead of allowing marriage to shape and bend us.

"WE KIND OF HAVE TO BELIEVE WHAT HE BELIEVES"

When I consider the selfless ideal of biblical marriage, I think of Allan Edwards, the pastor of Kiski Valley Presbyterian Church in western Pennsylvania. Allan is married to Leeanne, whom he met as a teenager at a Christian summer camp. They have a loving marriage and just had their first child.

What makes Allan unusual is that he struggled with same-sex attraction starting in high school and even considered finding a church that affirmed same-sex relationships. In the end, though, Allan had the courage not to fool himself. "I studied different methods of reading the Scripture, and it all came down to this: Jesus accepts the rest of the Scripture as divined from God. So if Jesus is who he says he is, then we kind of have to believe what he believes." Allan is right. "Everybody has this experience of wanting something else or beyond what they have. Everybody struggles with discontentment. The difference, I think, and the blessing Leeanne and I have experienced, is that we came into our marriage relationship already knowing and talking about it. And I think that's a really powerful basis for intimacy."

How many of us are willing to admit to having a similar struggle? No, I'm not attracted to other men, but I would be lying if I said I don't ever find other women attractive, and I'm hardly alone. The Scriptures tell us, "Flee from sexual immorality" (1 Cor. 6:18, ESV) and "Walk by the Spirit, and you will not gratify the desires of the flesh" (Gal. 5:16, ESV). Fortunately, Paul assures us, "No temptation has overtaken you that is not common to man," and "God is faithful, and he will not let you be tempted beyond your ability, but with temptation he will also provide the way of escape, that you may be able to endure it" (1 Cor. 10:13, ESV).

What I so admire about Allan's testimony is that he shows what it means to bridle our passion with biblical truth. Boldly and deliberately, he affirms that it's not about satisfying our impulses or desires but living obediently under the authority of the Holy Scriptures.

THE COST OF THE SIN OF SELFISHNESS

The psychological and spiritual cost of this selfishness is incalculable. But what about the economic cost? Does sexual freedom pay?

A researcher at Brigham Young University recently analyzed the economic costs of divorce to individuals, communities, and government and determined it was approximately $33.3 billion annually in the United States alone.[6] The Institute for American Values studied the same question but included the financial implications of children born outside of marriage. The researchers estimated (conservatively) that the financial burden is $112 billion annually, explaining, "These costs arise from increased taxpayer expenditures for antipoverty, criminal justice, and education programs, and through lower levels of taxes paid by individuals who, as adults, earn less because of reduced opportunities as a result of having been more likely to grow up in poverty."[7]

What *hasn't* been calculated, because it's impossible to determine, is the cost of marriages that never happen. Given all the good that healthy marriages generate, what have we lost as a result of so many couples' forgoing marriage altogether? Marriage serves four purely secular purposes that all societies require to thrive:

1. Marriage regulates sexuality.
2. Marriage domesticates and socializes men. It is the only way society has found to tie men cooperatively to their children.
3. Marriage protects women from male sexual exploitation and opportunism.
4. Marriage gives children the love, care, and provision of their own mother and father.

Think about any major social problem, where the state must step in to fill the gap, pick up the pieces, or fix the problem. Chances are it's the result of one or more of these legs of the stool being kicked out. The economist Lawrence Kudlow, observing that the dramatic slowdown in America's economic growth since 2002 has occurred under both Republican and Democrat presidents and Congresses, is convinced that a major cause of our economic weakness is the decline of marriage. "While restoring economic growth may be the great challenge of our time," he writes, "this goal will never be realized until we restore marriage."[8]

STATES WITH HIGHER MARRIAGE RATES ARE HEALTHIER

Show me a thriving community and I guarantee that you'll find thriving marriages. And communities without a healthy marriage culture will suffer from social dysfunction. The American Enterprise Institute and the Institute for Family Studies issued a report in 2015 titled *Strong Families, Prosperous States*, whose findings confirm common sense:

> Strong families can increase economic well-being because marriage and parenthood motivate men to work harder, more strategically, and more successfully, and to avoid behaviors—such as drinking to excess and criminal activity—that might limit their prospects at work. Both boys and girls raised in intact, married homes are likely to acquire more human capital—that is, more of the skills, habits, and values conducive to personal and economic success—and have access to more social capital (meaning institutions and groups that connect members with educational resources, job opportunities, and other benefits) than their peers in unmarried or unstable households. And families headed by married parents are likely to enjoy higher levels of income and assets and to gain more from economies of scale than single-parent families. Extending this logic to the macro level, we should expect larger shares of married adults and families headed by married parents

> to generate greater growth rates, higher rates of economic mobility, lower rates of childhood poverty, and higher levels of median family income at the state level.[9]

The breakdown of marriage, says Robert Putnam, a political scientist at Harvard, drives inequality between "children born to educated parents who are more likely to read to them as babies, to drive them to dance class, to nudge them into college themselves—and children whose parents live at the edge of economic survival."[10] The children of those parents who are fighting to survive, who live in virtual isolation, are in trouble, facing almost impossible obstacles on the road to success and opportunity.

My heart goes out to those kids because I was one of them, and I've had to struggle against feelings of guilt that I escaped while so many others did not. My past fuels my passion for God's design for families, driving me to stress the importance of marriage as a way to help eradicate poverty. Unmarried childbearing is the fastest road to poverty for moms and children, followed by cohabitation and divorce.

The numbers tell a sad story. In a given year, 15 percent of married couples are unable to meet utilities, food, and rent payments, but that figure doubles to 30 percent for cohabiting couples. Among singles with no other adult in the picture, it shoots up to 36 percent. If we reduce the divorce rate, we will inevitably reduce poverty. Some argue that this approach is flawed, that our culture is hopelessly "post-marriage," and that we should focus on the purely economic causes of poverty. But the solution to the problem isn't "either-or." Still, I would contend—and the data and experience show this to be true—that robust marriages are a more productive solution than robust social support.

Since President Johnson declared a war on poverty in 1964, nearly $22 trillion in taxpayer funds has been spent on it,[11] a conspicuous failure. Yet proposals to encourage marriage usually face opposition from government bureaucrats and politicians. It's therefore up to the rest of us to pour ourselves into the task of strengthening families by promoting the beauty and sanctity of marriage.

At Focus on the Family, that has become our magnificent obsession. In 2015, our resources helped 830,000 couples build stronger marriages and our efforts to help couples in crisis helped save more than 140,000 marriages. I will continue to extend invitations to other organizations, even those with whom we may not fully agree, to join us as we work to help families. Poverty is that important, and we can't afford to be hamstrung by partisanship. Poverty, single parenting, and divorce aren't Republican or Democratic problems. That's why the work we do—giving singles the tools they need to establish healthy marriages, offering couples in crisis hope and help to save their marriages, and equipping parents to raise thriving children—isn't "red" or "blue."

PRACTICAL WAYS WE CAN WORK TOGETHER

The AEI-IFS report on the correlation between healthy families and healthy states proposes several ways that society can strengthen marriages, including:

- Eliminate the "marriage penalty" in welfare programs that are based on a family's financial resources.
- Improve vocational education and increase the number of apprenticeships that are available, especially for young men.
- Enact divorce reforms that encourage couples to give their marriage another try, such as extending the waiting period before granting divorce if abuse, abandonment, or substance abuse is not a factor, as well as offering strong education programs that promote reconciliation.

- Consider education and civic campaigns to get young adults to follow the "success sequence" of getting an education, finding a job, and marrying before they start having children.

MARRIAGE IS THE BEST PROTECTION AGAINST FOUR ENEMIES

"Marriage has public purposes that transcend its private purposes," writes Ryan Anderson, one of the institution's ablest defenders in the public square.[12] Anyone who cares about equity and social justice simply *has* to take an interest in the outcome of the marriage debate. As the family goes, so goes society. In fact, strong marriages and intact families are our best defense against four of modern society's most pernicious enemies:

1. Persistent poverty

As Robert Putnam has pointed out, sixty years ago parental unemployment was the primary indicator of childhood poverty. Forty years ago, it was a lack of education. Both of these factors remain important, but most scholars today agree that marriage and family cohesion play a fundamental role in driving *every* important measure of social well-being. Isabel Sawhill of the Brookings Institution explains, "The proliferation of single-parent households accounts for virtually all of the increase in child poverty since the early 1970s."[13] President Barack Obama agrees: "We have too many children in poverty in this country, and everybody should be ashamed, but don't tell me it doesn't have a little to do with the fact that we got too many daddies not acting like daddies."[14]

2. Domestic, sexual, and physical violence

According to the U.S. Department of Justice, married women are more than three times less likely to become victims of violence than women who are single, cohabiting, or divorced.[15] The same source reports that domestic violence among intimate partners is dramatically lower among married spouses than among couples who are living together or dating—only 33 percent as compared with 50 percent.[16] And research published in the journal *Child Abuse and Neglect* found that a girl is seven times more likely to be molested by her stepfather than by her biological father.[17] Clearly, the best way to protect ourselves against violence in the home is to promote traditional marriage.

3. Educational failure

Numerous studies show that children living apart from their married mother and father are 50 to 80 percent more likely to do poorly in school than children living with both parents. They also drop out at a greater rate, have more behavioral problems with teachers and other students, and are less likely to attend or graduate from college. As Professor Putnam observes, "The... [growing] gap is created more by what happens to kids *before* they get to school... than by what schools do to them. The American public school today is a kind of echo chamber in which the advantages or disadvantages that children bring with them to the classroom are academically magnified."[18]

4. Crime

Boys raised in single-parent homes are about twice as likely—and those raised in stepfamilies are two and a half times more likely—to commit crimes than those raised by both biological parents.[19] William Galston and Elaine Kamarck of the Progressive Policy Institute conclude that the relationship between crime and fatherless families is "so strong that controlling for family configuration erases the relationship between race and crime and between low income and crime."[20]

The message in these data is as plain as day. Strong marriages build better homes. And stronger homes produce healthier children who grow up to be healthier and more productive adults. What makes this message all the more impressive is that it has the endorsement of researchers from *both* ends of the political spectrum. Their voices are unanimous. If we want to beat poverty, crime, violence, and educational failure, we've got to preserve traditional marriage and protect the institution of the family.

PART II

Your Marriage

CHAPTER NINE

The Sanctity of Sex

Those who have never known the deep intimacy and the intense companionship of mutual love have missed the best thing that life has to give.

—Bertrand Russell

A recent issue of *Reader's Digest* grabbed my attention. Splashed across the front cover was the question "Is Your Marriage Normal or Nuts?"[1] The article promised to share "8 Lessons from the World's Happiest Couples." Naturally, I was intrigued. Jean and I would consider ourselves part of a happy marriage. But could we vouch for all eight of these "lessons"?

The list was fairly predictable. Happily married couples are kind to each other and talk regularly about all kinds of things. They also avoid going to bed angry. But, speaking of bed, this one really jumped out at me: According to the experts associated with the *Reader's Digest* study, 60 percent of extremely happy couples have sex three or four times per week.[2] I had to read that statistic again. *Three or four times per week*?

My first thought was that I wanted to share the article with Jean, and years ago I would have done so. I'm not quite so clueless now, though. I'm certain she would have noted that the majority of those "extremely happy" women were not mothers of young children, which she is. It's not that moms of youngsters aren't interested in sexual intimacy, but the minute they lie down they're likely to fall asleep out of sheer exhaustion. In this season of life, Jean is going a hundred miles an hour, investing in the lives of our young boys. A *Reader's Digest* sex life will have to wait!

Yet intimacy doesn't have to be a casualty of the daily grind. Bill and Pam Farrel, frequent guests on the Focus on the Family radio program, are adept at guiding couples through the challenging waters of sexual intimacy and helping them set and adjust their expectations. And when it comes to the issue of couples' prioritizing special time together, Bill and Pam have strong opinions:

> [As married couples] we must make a choice regarding sexual expression. We will either utilize it as a deviant, destructive power or we will harness its potential to keep love alive and vibrant in our marriage relationships. In marriage, sex is the spice that rescues our relationships from becoming mundane pursuits of chores. Adult life is filled with responsibilities. We have mortgages to pay, yard work to maintain, laundry to clean, cars to service, and so on. But none of us got married so we could load up on chores. We got married out of hope. We got married because we believed there was some kind of magic between us. We got married because we believed we could have great sex together.
>
> A satisfying sex life can add dignity to all other pursuits of life. It is the thing to look forward to after a dull or

> miserable day at work. Sex is the moment of connection that creates a deep bond, even when sprinkled weeks or months apart. Sexual union adds an underlying deposit of strength that can help hold couples together when life threatens to pull them apart.[3]

Sadly, the confusion about sex and sexuality that is rampant in our culture has spread to the Christian community. God's design for sexual intimacy is too important for the Church to politely ignore. If we don't care for it, you can be certain that the world and the devil will corrupt it. To be sure, our emotional and physical desire for sex is God-given. It's wired into us, designed to be fulfilled in the loving relationship of marriage.

The trouble, though, is that a lot of things, like the demands of parenthood, can interfere with a fulfilling sexual relationship between husband and wife. The demands of children can sap a woman of the energy she needs for intimacy with her husband. By the end of the day, many women feel they have nothing left to give to their husbands.

Another kind of challenge is that some Christian women find it hard to redefine their understanding of sex once they're married. Throughout adolescence, they're told *no, no, no*, but as soon as they're married, it becomes *yes, yes, yes*. That can be a difficult transition. Some women grow up with the message that sex is bad. Instead of looking forward to it, some actually dread it. I've heard stories of Christian women hating every minute of their honeymoon, feeling guilty and dirty because they were doing something they had been taught to believe "good girls don't do." And it can go beyond the first week or two. Some find it incredibly difficult to "flip the switch" even months or years into their marriage.

Other couples enter marriage with a distorted view of sex. Intimacy brings out their insecurities—the fear that they're not pretty enough, not thin enough, or not good enough to please their spouse. For intimacy to thrive in their marriages, men and women have to learn how to integrate their sexuality with their faith, making it a healthy part of their relationship with their spouse. It's about knowing the person God created you to be and living it out.

THE BIBLE AND SEX

When couples ask us at Focus on the Family what the Scriptures have to say about sex within marriage, we tell them the Bible has three important things to say about the meaning and purpose of marital sex. First, it is central to the process by which husband and wife become *one flesh* (Gen. 2:24). In this day and age, one often has to point out the obvious, as when Rick Warren explained on *Larry King Live* that men and women are anatomically complementary—the parts fit! That's obviously not the case with couples of the same sex. Second, the Bible suggests marital sex is the means whereby man and woman participate in the ongoing work of God's creation (Gen. 1:28). Again, two men alone or two women alone cannot conceive a child. Third, sex within marriage symbolizes the union between Christ and His Church (Eph. 5:31–32). Sex, then, isn't "all about me." From first to last, it is part of the give-and-take of an interpersonal *relationship*. It is a holy mystery, a powerful bonding agent that shapes the relationship between a man and a woman as nothing else can.

Given the biblical purposes of sex, Christian married couples might wonder what's appropriate within the bedroom, especially since men and women are wired differently and spouses may have very different backgrounds. Certain theological perspectives and biblical principles should inform a married couple's expression of physical intimacy. Marriage is a relationship of love in which a man and a woman model for each other Christ's self-sacrificial love for His

Church. Where there is love, there is liberty, but love also demands respect for the needs, feelings, and desires of one's mate. The pleasure that accompanies the marital embrace is God's gift and is therefore good—even holy. There is no shame in its enjoyment. But if we pursue that pleasure merely for its own sake, we contradict the mutual and complete gift of self—body and spirit—that is the essence of marriage and consummated in the conjugal act.

It's important to remember that sexual intimacy in marriage is a lifelong process. Its expression will vary in youth and old age, in times of stress and times of joy, during pregnancy, childbirth, and child-rearing, during and after menopause—the list could go on and on. At every stage, healthy attitudes toward marital sex are characterized by candor, prayerfulness, vulnerability, flexibility, and willingness to communicate.

THE DIFFERENCE BETWEEN LOVE AND SEX

Do you think most married couples know the difference between love and sex? I can't speak for every man, but I suspect a lot of men assume they have that distinction pretty well settled—until they realize the lines are more blurred than they thought, and their marriage suffers because of it. Problems with sex and intimacy in marriage are among the top reasons people contact us at Focus on the Family. The question of love and sex is far more complicated than most people realize when they first get married. In fact, many younger couples enter marriage thinking of sex and love as the "easy" part of their relationship. Isn't that how Hollywood portrays it? They have no idea as yet how delicately love and sex are intertwined and little appreciation for their power to enrich or destroy a marriage. The challenges to marital intimacy are numberless and unending, from unrealistic expectations and busy schedules to the demands of children and the infirmities of old age.

ADVICE OLD AND NEW

It is easy to be so consumed by our own world of troubles—whether in our marriage, in parenting, or in our professional work—that we forget that every problem we face has, in some form or fashion, also been a problem for prior generations. Nowhere is this truer than in marriage and the sexual realm. In my research for this book, I reviewed numerous old pamphlets and books of marital advice. The oldest is a document from ancient China, *circa* 300 BC, found in a tomb. The topics addressed include "Four Seasons of Sex and Why Autumn Is Hot, Hot, Hot," "Wild New Positions," "Aphrodisiacs to Keep You Up All Night!," and "Your Love Route to Immortality."[4]

Of course, much of the advice from years ago is dated, and some of it is downright crazy. *Becklard's Physiology: Physiological Mysteries and Revelations in Love, Courtship and Marriage: An Infallible Guide-Book for Married and Single Persons, in Matters of the Utmost Importance to the Human Race*, published in the 1850s, counseled that "the party whose temperament predominates in the child was in the highest state of orgasm at the period of intercourse."[5] In *Sexual Health: A Plain and Practical Guide for the People on All Matters concerning the Organs of Reproduction in Both Sexes and All Ages* (1887), Dr. Henry Hanchett urged married couples to engage in sexual relations every three days. If they waited any longer, Hanchett warned, "The children propagated from these unions would grow to be shriveled and unhealthy since their parents didn't express enough love."[6]

For all the amusingly antiquated physiology, I discovered some real food for thought in the marital manuals of yesteryear. Edward Podolsky's *Sex Today in Wedded Life* (1947)[7] offers this advice:

Ten Commandments for Wives

1. Don't bother your husband with petty troubles and complaints when he comes home from work.

2. Be a good listener. Let him tell you his troubles; yours will seem trivial in comparison.
3. Remember your most important job is to build up and maintain his ego (which gets bruised plenty in business). Morale is a woman's business.
4. Let him relax before dinner, and discuss family problems after the "inner man" has been satisfied.
5. Always remember he's a male and marital relations promote harmony. Have sane views about sex.
6. No man likes a wife who is always tired out. Conserve your energy so you can give him the companionship he craves.
7. Never hold up your husband to ridicule in the presence of others. If you must criticize, do so privately and without anger.
8. Remember a man is only a grown-up boy. He needs mothering and enjoys it if not piled on too thick.
9. Don't live beyond your means, or add to your husband's financial burdens.
10. Don't try to boss him around. Let him think he wears the pants.

Did you pick up on the last one? "Let him *think* he wears the pants." Who said some advice isn't timeless? Now let's take a look at the advice for husbands:

Ten Commandments for Husbands

1. Remember your wife wants to be treated as your sweetheart always.
2. Remember her birthdays and your wedding anniversaries.
3. Bring her some gift every week, no matter how inexpensive it may be. (It's not the price, it's the thought.)

4. Don't take love for granted. Don't "ration" your kisses. Being a woman, she wants you to woo her.
5. Respect her privacy.
6. Always be tender, kind and considerate even under trying circumstances.
7. Don't be stingy with money; be a generous provider.
8. Compliment her new dress, "hair-do," cooking, etc.
9. Always greet her with a kiss, especially when other people are around.
10. Remember marriage is a 50-50 proposition and you are not the majority stock holder.

Now, some of Podolsky's commandments sound as dated as a buggy whip—a wife's troubles "will seem trivial in comparison" with her husband's!—but some of them are perfectly timeless. For example, it's tempting for some, especially women, to treat sex as merely another item on a never-ending to-do list. But Podolsky understood that it's wise not to do that. With good communication, intentionality, and some creativity, you *can* keep the flame of intimacy burning in your marriage, whatever your stage of life. To help you do that, I have collected some wise advice from Focus on the Family's counselors and marriage experts to help you and your spouse prioritize the sexual portion of your marriage.

1. Take the long view

When you look at marriage as a lifelong commitment with implications for your eternal destiny, you gain a better perspective of the stage you're in at the moment. It won't always be like this. Take a big, deep breath and remember the words of the Apostle James: "Yet you do not know what your life will be like tomorrow. You are just a vapor that appears for a little while and then vanishes away" (James 4:14, NASB). I don't want to minimize your challenges, but in view of eternity, are your sexual frustrations worth jeopardizing your relationship with the Lord over? Of course not.

2. You can experience intimacy in a variety of ways

There's more to marriage than sexual intercourse—although that is important too. It is helpful to remember that although fatigue, stress, and busyness may affect your sex life, you can still strive for intimacy. If you're creative, you can come up with a thousand ways to connect emotionally without being physical. Respect each other's varied ways of feeling and experiencing romance and try to serve both needs equally. You can enjoy a cup of coffee on your deck, snuggle on the couch while you watch TV, or have a heart-to-heart conversation in the car as the kids snooze in the backseat.

3. Keep the boundaries around the marriage strong through intentional measures

While sex shouldn't become the ultimate pursuit in a marriage, it still is an important part of it. God created sex as a way a husband and wife can become one, and it strengthens their marital bond. Couples need to find time for sexual intimacy, and for some it even makes sense to schedule times for it. We make time for dentist appointments and soccer practice—why not sex? Being open to spontaneity is also a good habit, especially for the very busy parent. If your children are young, why not establish earlier bedtimes for the kids? This will give you some built-in "together time" for each other every day. The Apostle Paul cautioned married Christians to "not deprive one another...so that Satan may not tempt you because of your lack of self-control" (1 Cor. 7:5, ESV). Do you and your spouse have a date night? Our research tells us that 92 percent of couples who make date night a priority have increased satisfaction in their relationships.

4. Understanding and patience foster an environment where sex is a possibility

Couples should treat each other well not as a means to an end but because that's the right thing to do—but that doesn't mean that we can't enjoy the benefits if we do what's right. Husbands, your wife may feel overwhelmed at having to keep up with the kids and the house, so pitch in and help. Many wives who previously didn't have an "acts of service" love language might develop it during the baby and toddler years.

COMMUNICATION IS KEY

How frequently should a married couple expect to be sexually intimate? There's no right answer to this question. When I polled our radio audience, the responses were, predictably, all over the map, ranging from once a month to four or five times per week. Our counselors will tell you that complaints about infrequent sexual intimacy are usually masking a deeper problem, such as a failure to communicate. Many a wife notices a marked improvement in her husband's communication skills when he's interested in sex. We must continually evaluate our habits and motives. Of course, infrequency of intimacy can be the result of fatigue. If you're the parent of a toddler or consumed with the stresses and strains of a busy professional life outside the house, you might be too tired and busy even to think about sex with your spouse, and for good reason—your sleep schedule is off.

If that's where you're at these days, talking about sex with your spouse, as difficult as that might be, is critical. Resentment can develop quickly when one spouse expects one thing and the other expects something else. Writing in the *Wall Street Journal*, Elizabeth Bernstein offers some practical guidelines for discussing your sex life with your spouse:

- Be gentle. Need an opening line? "I love you, and I'd like to feel more connected to you."

- Never discuss sex right after having sex (unless you have only good things to say). Sex therapists say the best place to discuss sex is out of the bedroom—in the kitchen while making dinner, on a walk, taking a drive.
- Realize that the discussion may take more than one conversation. You don't have to knock it out all in one sitting.
- Don't ascribe blame. Don't psychoanalyze. Just describe what you feel is the problem. "You seem much less interested in sex than you used to be." Ask if your partner has noticed this as well.[8]

One of the most insightful experts in this field is Dr. Juli Slattery, the president and cofounder of Authentic Intimacy, a ministry dedicated to "reclaiming God's design for intimacy and sexuality," and the author of three exceptionally helpful books.[9] With her husband, Mike, she does her best to address the kinds of issues married people grapple with but rarely talk about. Juli has written for Focus on the Family about the sensitivity and sacredness of marital sexual intimacy, and it's so helpful that I'm going to share it here:

How Will You Respond to the Challenges You Face?

You must determine now what kind of lover you will be. How will you respond to the inevitable disappointments and discouragements of sexual love? Will the challenges prove that you are quick to hold a grudge or eager to forgive? Defensive or humble? Selfish or sacrificial? Demanding or sensitive?

The best advice I can give you is to determine to be a team in sexual intimacy, no matter what. God has given you sex not just for pleasure and procreation, but also to glue you together in profound ways. Sexual oneness isn't just about naked bodies touching, but eventually demands that your love is tested and shared with vulnerability and authentic intimacy.

Here are four practical suggestions—things that are true of every great team and all great lovers:

1. Great teams communicate with each other. Talking about sexual intimacy can be a challenge. To start with, what words do you use to describe sexual acts, desires, and the sexual parts of the body? The words you like might be offensive to your husband or wife. Or maybe you just feel awkward talking about the whole topic.

Sexual conversations can quickly escalate into raw conflict. Why? Because sexuality is so core to who you are as a person. It's humiliating to admit to a porn struggle. It's embarrassing to ask your spouse for more sex and devastating to hear that you are not meeting your husband's or wife's sexual needs. Sexual conflict usually taps into issues of shame, control, body image, trust, masculinity, and femininity. A lot of couples choose not to venture into this emotional minefield, so they just avoid the topic.

It doesn't take a psychologist to figure out that you can't solve problems together if you don't communicate. You can't learn to please each other if the very topic is off-limits. So, how do you learn to talk about sex together?

- *Let someone else start the conversation.* When Mike and I encountered this roadblock, we used things like books, marriage seminars, and radio broadcasts to bring up the topics that we didn't know how to address. When authors like Cliff and Joyce Penner explained a common problem, I could just say, "I feel like they just described." These outside resources gave us the permission and the words to start the conversation.

- *Make sexual conversations safe.* I can think of at least a handful of times that I hurt Mike with insensitive words on this topic. Sometimes it was a flippant remark; other times my cutting words came out of my own hurt. Be aware that your spouse is probably very sensitive about sexual issues, just as you are. Ask questions and listen. His or her perspective is very different from yours, so don't assume anything. If you have a "complaint," share it with grace, remembering that you are both just learning how to love one another.

2. Great teams have solid coaching. If talking about sex with your spouse is difficult, try admitting a sexually related problem to a doctor, therapist, or pastor. Yes, that's exactly what might be required to get through challenges like a sexual addiction, physical problems, infertility, or healing from sexual abuse.

I've seen couples stop having sex at all because the husband or wife was too embarrassed to get help. A great sexual relationship will require you to fight through barriers. At times, this will mean admitting that you need help. Getting married, establishing a sexual relationship with your spouse, and even having children can trigger wounds and memories of sexual trauma for both men and women. It will be very difficult to move forward in intimacy in marriage without addressing past trauma.

As a psychologist, I've had the privilege of working with many marriages through difficulties related to intimacy. I have the greatest respect for a man or woman who is willing to ask for help and engage in the healing process. If you have sexual trauma in your past or think you have a sexual addiction, please don't try to convince yourself that your wounds will go away. The great news is that God is the Healer, even of sexual pain. His truth can set you free from lies, His peace can calm your anxiety, His forgiveness can cleanse the darkest sin, and His love can be a healing balm over violation and betrayal. (Refer to *Surprised by the Healer.*[10])

3. Great teams never confuse a teammate for the opponent. Sexual temptation is nothing new. Just read Proverbs, which was written thousands of years ago, and you will see that even then, men were strongly warned to avoid the deception of an alluring harlot. While you could find illicit sex thousands of years ago, now it is actively pursuing you—whether you are male or female, married or single.

Almost every man and many women will enter marriage with some history with pornography or erotica (often the female version of porn). Because of their widespread use, visual and written porn are often just accepted as a fact of life. But just because something is accepted as normal doesn't mean it isn't also deadly.

Satan hates marriage and despises the beauty of sexual oneness. He constantly attempts to destroy, demolish, and distort married sex. Not only will he use sexual temptation to water down your sexual intimacy, he will try to use the battle to divide you. One of his most successful strategies is to turn husband and wife against each other.

Battling sexual temptation is difficult enough, but it becomes impossible when you are fighting each other instead of clearly identifying the true enemy.

Regardless of which of you struggles with sexual temptation, you must begin to see this as your problem as a couple. I do not mean that a wife should take responsibility for her husband's purity or vice versa. However, when sexual sin and temptation hit one of you, they impact both of you. Satan will use pornography, inappropriate emotional attachments, and other forms of temptation to further divide you if he can define your spouse as "the problem" or "the enemy." As long as you are fighting each other, you cannot stand together. Standing together starts with humility and empathy. As Jesus taught, we cannot lovingly confront another person's sin until we have brought our own failings before God's grace. You might not know what it is like to struggle with sexual temptation, but you do know what it's like to have a "besetting sin." Maybe yours is gossip, dishonesty, bitterness, pride, or coveting. Confront your spouse with the humility and awareness of your own weaknesses, rather than feeding shame with a self-righteous spirit of judgment.

Empathy doesn't mean that you ignore the problem, but that you strive together in God's strength to honor Him. The thing I love about this is it turns Satan's strategies against him. Instead of being divided, you and your spouse will become more united than ever as you fight together for your marriage. Indeed, God can "work all things together for the good of those who love God and are called according to His purpose."

4. Great teams play offense and defense. If you are a sports fan, you know the importance of a great offense and defense. No team can win a Super Bowl, World Series, NBA championship, or World Cup without both. The same is true in your marriage. For your love life to flourish and go the distance, you have to work together to build offensive and defensive strategies.

A lot of the information you get from Christian sources emphasizes defense. Many sermons and books teach about the importance of purity in marriage, setting up hedges against affairs, and battling temptation. Building boundaries and safeguards to keep your marriage bed pure is extremely important. You need to talk about things like whether to keep old flames as Facebook friends and what boundaries to have with opposite-sex coworkers.

Just as important as playing "defense," you need to work together to learn how to "score" (yes, the pun is intended). As they say in sports, "The best defense is a great offense." This definitely applies to married sexuality. A couple who has a mutually satisfying, exciting sex life is far less open to temptation than the couple who doesn't.

How do you create an exciting sex life in marriage? First, by realizing that you have permission to do so. A lot of Christians (particularly women) have a hard time erasing all of the "thou shalt not" messages. Even though you might intellectually know that it's OK to have sex, you still feel restrained or guilty being *too* sexual. Are Christians really supposed to get carried away with sexual pleasure in the marriage bed? The answer is "yes." If you don't believe me, take a look at the Song of Solomon. Both Solomon and his bride were very free with their bodies and their words and absolutely taken with sexual pleasure. And God said this was good!

John Piper encourages married couples to offensively battle Satan by pleasing each other in bed:

> A married couple gives a severe blow to the head of that ancient serpent when they aim to give as much sexual satisfaction to each other as possible. Is it not a

mark of amazing grace that on top of all the pleasure that the sexual side of marriage brings, it also proves to be a fearsome weapon against our ancient foe?[11]

There is nothing spiritual about settling for a mediocre sex life. Yes, there will be seasons of marriage in which sex might be difficult or may not be a high priority. But God's desire for you is that you continue to work toward experiencing the greatest sexual delight in one another. Building a great sex life over the years will take intentionality, time, and effort. It's well worth the effort and a whole lot more fun than just playing defense!

I love Juli's upbeat approach to this challenging yet beautiful part of marriage. Indeed, pursuing and maintaining sexual intimacy with our spouse can be one of the most enjoyable aspects of married life. Yes, the degree and frequency of physical intimacy can change with the seasons of life, but with good communication, intentionality, and some creativity, you can keep the flame of intimacy going for the duration of your marriage.

CHAPTER TEN

Remarriage and Starting Anew

This is life. Things get taken away. You will learn to start over many times—or you will be useless.[1]

—Mitch Albom

When Emily arrived in Colorado Springs in the late spring of 2000 to begin a new job at Focus on the Family, driving a compact car that contained all her possessions, she appeared to be your typical twenty-something professional. Only weeks earlier, she had graduated with honors from Southwestern Seminary in Fort Worth, Texas, with a master's degree in communication. A former professional musician, she settled into a studio apartment, eager to begin her job as a ministry publicist. With a strong testimony and a heart full of dreams, she was upbeat and excited.

She was also starting over.

Just four years earlier, Emily had found herself entangled in an abusive marriage to a young man who was not only unfaithful to her but also addicted to drugs. Counseling proved unsuccessful. Heartbroken, desperate, and far from home, she phoned her parents, unsure what to say and what to do. After only a few minutes of evasive but emotional conversation, Emily's father, a pastor, sensed something was terribly wrong. "Stay right where you are," he said. "Pack your bags. I'm coming to get you." Within twenty-four hours, Emily was back with her parents. Through tears, she would later recall the incident as "the night my father saved my life." Growing up in a conservative Christian home, she could hardly fathom this devastating turn of events. After all, marriage was for life. Divorce was never discussed as an option. But just two years on their journey to "forever together," everything had gone horribly wrong. What in the world had happened? Had she seen it coming? Yes, but she had lived in denial, hoping it would all somehow work out. It didn't. Within a year, the divorce was finalized. Emily would never see her former husband again.

Sadly, Emily's painful story is not unusual. The details vary, of course, but the prevalence of divorce is indisputable. With more than eight hundred thousand divorces in the United States in 2014,[2] we all know people who have been through the agony of a marital dissolution. You may be one of them. We often hear, moreover, that Christians divorce at the same rate as non-Christians, an embarrassing charge if true, since Christ Himself has decreed that marriage, with few exceptions, is for life. But is the charge true? On closer inspection, it turns out that the divorce rate for Christians who are actively practicing their faith (church attendance, bible study, and so on), while too high, is significantly lower than for people who merely claim church membership. Still, that's little solace when you find yourself a statistic.

So what became of Emily? After everything had fallen apart for her, she easily could have blamed her ex-husband and grown bitter. Instead, she did the opposite. "I realized," she says, "that although [my ex-husband] broke our vows and mistreated me, I needed to examine what it was about myself that led me to even fall for him in the first place. If I were to ever marry again, I was determined to not make the same mistakes." Emily learned a lot about herself in the next few years. She took a break from her music, went back to seminary, and decided not to date for a while. Her healing took time:

> My counselor helped me realize that I was afraid to be alone and that this thirst for company, for affirmation, was part of the reason I had made an unhealthy and unwise choice to get married while I was still in college. In doing so, I let him walk all over me. He mistreated me. That wasn't my fault. He's responsible for his actions. But I have to own my part of it all. I didn't have to take his insults and I didn't have to put up with his dishonesty. Counseling helped me see that I was looking for him to give me what only the Lord could provide. Over time, I realized that God was sufficient. Yes, I still had a desire to one day marry and even be a mom, but my priorities needed a major adjustment.

Five years from the lowest point in her life, Emily married Jason, another Focus staffer. Today, they're closing in on fifteen happy years together and are the proud parents of three young boys. "The Lord has redeemed those lost years from my first marriage," says Emily. "I wouldn't want to go through it again, but I would never trade what He taught me in the process. He gave me a second chance and an opportunity to start over again."

As the Smalley Institute says, people who are getting remarried should

> recognize what you did wrong in the first marriage and fix that immediately. You were not perfect, even if you were only at fault for 20 per cent of the problems in your first marriage. You need to spend 100 per cent of your time fixing that 20 per cent. Whatever dysfunction you had in the first marriage will not magically disappear in your second marriage. Negative patterns and behaviors have a way of repeating themselves. Your new marriage will have its own set of issues, so please do not bring in old issues.[3]

THE BIBLE, DIVORCE, AND REMARRIAGE

The question of divorce and remarriage is a contentious one for Christians. I believe the Bible is clear that God hates divorce (Mal. 2:16) and desires to bring healing, forgiveness, and reconciliation to broken marital relationships. Nevertheless, our understanding at Focus on the Family is that there are three situations in which the Scriptures make allowance for divorce and remarriage. The first is when a marriage and divorce occurred prior to salvation. Although a person cannot undo all the sins he has committed, he is forgiven for the wrongs he did before accepting Christ (see 2 Cor. 5:17). The second, which Jesus states specifically in Matthew 19:9, is when one's mate is guilty of sexual immorality and is unwilling to repent and live faithfully. And the third is when one of the spouses is an unbeliever and willfully and permanently deserts the believing partner. This refers not to a temporary departure but to a permanent abandonment (see 1 Cor. 7:12–15). To be clear, I think there's good reason to suppose that when Jesus makes allowance for divorce, He's simultaneously making allowance for remarriage—at least in certain cases. This seems to be reflected in Matthew 5:32: "Whoever divorces his wife for any reason except sexual immorality causes her to commit adultery. . . ." In other words, if the reason for the divorce is legitimate, there can be no grounds for labeling any subsequent remarriage as "adulterous."

In any case, I don't intend to dwell on the ins and outs of biblical theology. Many of my readers and their children are grappling with divorce, and I want to be helpful. At Focus on the Family, we're primarily in the business of ministering to moms, dads, and kids who need our assistance. Whether we like it or not, there are lots of second-marriage, blended families, many of whom identify themselves as evangelical Christians, and they're reaching out to us for help. We can't turn them away. I'm not encouraging anyone to get divorced and remarried. On the contrary, at Focus, we are and always will be committed to the sanctity and permanence of the marital bond. But we have to meet people where they are.

ANTICIPATING THE CHALLENGES

Ron Deal, the founder of Smart Stepfamilies,[4] an organization dedicated to helping remarried couples and stepfamilies, stresses the importance of assessing the reality of a situation, warning that we easily deceive ourselves. According to Ron's research, 75 percent of soon-to-be-remarried couples never discuss such important issues as their parenting or marriage expectations. Assuming everything will work out simply because you love each other is not a recipe for success. Ron suggests meeting with a counselor to assess individual strengths and weaknesses: "Couples need to step away from their remarriage fantasies and consider the realities of stepfamily life. In order to make a step in the right direction for you and your children, you first must understand the challenges of stepfamily living and then make an informed choice about remarriage."[5]

The *Wall Street Journal*'s Elizabeth Bernstein asked marriage experts for their best advice for those considering a second (or third) marriage. Many of the answers she received mirror the advice we give at Focus:

> Spend some time being single. Explore conflicts you have in relationships of all types, preferably with a therapist's help. Ask yourself what it's like to live with you.
>
> Figure out why you want to be married. Is it financial security? A father or mother for your kids? A new life? Make a list of what you really want—and don't want—from remarriage. What will you give up and what do you hope to gain? Does your new partner provide what you need—or are you simply trying not to be alone?...
>
> Give your partner space to be with his or her children alone. Talk about who will make parenting decisions.
>
> Make sure your new partner will agree to couples therapy if necessary....[6]

Michael Smalley, another son of the late relationship guru Gary Smalley and the brother of my colleague Greg, concurs:

> If you're starting over, please understand the necessity for getting counseling with your new mate to learn the skills it takes to have a satisfying marriage. You're going to have to learn new ways of interacting with your spouse, or you'll tend to simply fall back into the old ways of interacting, which led to your first divorce. We know today what it takes to have a successful and satisfying relationship; it's not a mystery. There are specific skills that, if applied, can actually eliminate your chances of divorce. Couples who

> receive premarital training increase their chances of staying married for a lifetime almost 80 per cent![7]

Les and Leslie Parrott also stress the importance of addressing chronic personal defects:

> Recognize what you did wrong in the first marriage and fix that immediately. You were not perfect [in your previous marriage]. Much of your personal readiness for remarriage depends on the state of your relationship with your former spouse, whether they are deceased or you are divorced. What lessons from your first marriage will you bring into your second marriage? Is there unresolved pain in relation to your first spouse that you still need to work through? The point is that before reentering marriage, you need to carefully examine the baggage you are bringing with you.[8]

If you'd like a referral for a counselor in your area or a recommendation for an online assessment tool, I encourage you to contact us at Focus on the Family. Whether it's through the Parrotts or Focus on the Family's Hope Restored program in Branson, Missouri, we want to get you the help you need.

STEPFAMILY SUCCESS

Is it possible to have a successful and happy second marriage? Of course it is. One of my favorite examples has to be Ronald Reagan's marriage to Nancy Davis, whom he wed in 1952. Although Reagan had told his first wife, the actress Jane Wyman, "I believe we belong together and that we will end our days together," their marriage ended after only eight years.[9] Though Hollywood gossip writers and close friends saw the divorce coming for years, Reagan himself was crushed when Wyman packed his bags and loaded them into his convertible. "I suppose there had been warning signs," he reflected, "if only I hadn't been too busy, but small-town boys grow up thinking only other people get divorced. The plain truth was that such a thing was so far from ever being imagined by me that I had no resources to call on."[10] Years later, looking back on the sad turn of events that eventually would lead him to a successful fifty-two-year marriage, Ronald Reagan would call his first divorce a lucky defeat.

Reagan, the president of the Screen Actors Guild, met Nancy in 1951 when she enlisted his help in untangling a mess she found herself in. Another actress by the same name had been placed on the notorious McCarthy-era Hollywood blacklist of communist sympathizers, and the future first lady was having difficulty landing roles. Reagan obliged, and the two quickly fell in love. Charlton Heston, a good friend of the Reagans, called their marriage "probably the greatest love affair in the history of the American presidency."[11] On their thirty-first wedding anniversary, in 1983, President Reagan wrote, "Dear First Lady.... You know I love the ranch but these last two days made it plain I only love it when you are there. Come to think of it that's true of every place & every time. When you aren't there I'm no place, just lost in time & space. I more than love you, I'm not whole without you. You are life itself to me. When you are gone I'm waiting for you to return so I can start living again."[12] Expressing the same feeling, Nancy wrote, "If either of us left the room, we both felt lonely. People didn't always believe this, but it's true. Filling the loneliness, completing each other—that's what it still meant to us to be husband and wife."[13]

Having endured the pain of a failed marriage and knowing the joy of a happy one, Reagan shared some frank and fatherly advice on the occasion of his son Michael's wedding in 1971:

> Some men feel their masculinity can only be proven if they play out in their own life all the locker-room stories, smugly confident that what a wife doesn't know won't hurt her. The truth is, somehow, way down inside, without her ever finding lipstick on the collar or catching a man in the flimsy excuse of where he was till three a.m., a wife does know, and with that knowing, some of the magic of this relationship disappears. There are more men griping about marriage who kicked the whole thing away themselves than there can ever be wives deserving of blame.
>
> There is an old law of physics that you can only get out of a thing as much as you put in it. The man who puts into the marriage only half of what he owns will get that out.... [L]et me tell you how really great is the challenge of proving your masculinity and charm with one woman for the rest of your life.
>
> ...If you truly love a girl, you shouldn't ever want her to feel, when she sees you greet a secretary or a girl you both know, that humiliation of wondering if she was someone who caused you to be late coming home, nor should you want any other woman to be able to meet your wife and know she was smiling behind her eyes as she looked at her, the woman you love, remembering this was the woman you rejected even momentarily for her favors.

The future president added the postscript, "You'll never get in trouble if you say 'I love you' at least once a day."[14]

My boys are still many years from marriage, but I need to remember to put down on paper some of the "secrets" to a happy married life that Ronald Reagan shared with his son. I encourage you to do the same.

TEN RULES FOR A HAPPY SECOND MARRIAGE

The Good Men Project, a multimedia enterprise dedicated to starting "an international conversation about what it means to be a good man in the twenty-first century," has identified "Ten Rules for a Happy Second Marriage," which, with their permission, I'd like to share with you:

1. Practice being vulnerable in small steps so you can build confidence in being more open with your partner. Discussing minor issues (schedules, meals) is a great place to start before tackling bigger matters such as disciplining kids or finances.
2. Honesty and communication are key issues in a second marriage. Be sure to be forthcoming about finances, your past, and concerns with your former spouse and children that are relevant.
3. Practice forgiveness. Forgiveness isn't the same as condoning the hurt done to you, but it will allow you to move on. Try to remember you are on the same team.
4. Take time as a couple to do things you enjoy without your children. A "date night" or couples time can be very enriching—even if it's a walk or grabbing a sandwich at a restaurant together.
5. Express thoughts, feelings, and wishes in a respectful way. Resentment can build when couples sweep things under the rug, so be vulnerable and don't bury negative feelings.
6. Discuss hot-button issues such as money and personality conflicts privately—but hold regular, informal family meetings (where everyone feels heard) to clear the air and address family issues.

7. Don't let differences in child rearing come between you. The role of the stepparent is one of a friend and supporter rather than a disciplinarian. Learn new strategies and share your ideas.
8. Accept that there will be inevitable ups and downs. Try to be more understanding with each other—and your children and stepchildren.
9. Don't make ultimatums such as "I'm leaving if things don't improve." Take the "D" word out of your vocabulary. According to renowned researcher E. Mavis Hetherington, seeing divorce as an option and talking about it can increase your risks for breakup.
10. Make a commitment to practice endurance and patience. In time, many of the kinks inherent in stepfamily life will smooth out.[15]

A WORD ABOUT STEPFAMILIES

The subject of stepfamilies is close to my heart. When my mother remarried after divorcing my father, I fantasized about having a father like Ward Cleaver from *Leave It to Beaver*, a kind and gentle leader who would shepherd me through adolescence and the twists and turns of life. I imagined him cheering me on from the stands or standing beside me in a sunlit river, fishing poles in hand. Instead, I got "Hank the Tank"—an ex-military officer who, though he loved my mother, never warmed up to her children. If I made a mistake, he would come down hard on me. Once, when I forgot to hang up my coat, he made me take it up and down off the hook five hundred times. Hank was married to my mom about a year and a half before she died, and the day of the funeral, he walked out on us. He said he couldn't take the pressure.

My unhappy experience has sensitized me to the challenges children face when families are blended together, but I also know that Hank wasn't the typical stepparent. Many of them quietly sacrifice themselves for their spouse's children, whom they try to treat as their own, sometimes with little thanks from those children, who have been badly hurt by divorce. Perhaps you are a stepparent, or maybe you were raised by one. Don't forget that God understands the struggles as well as your innermost thoughts. He is aware of the challenges you face. He is always available for you. He loves you.

All stepparents deserve our love and need our prayers. I hope you'll consider offering a word of encouragement to a stepmom or stepdad today. Their lives can be difficult. You might think you know what's going on in another person's life, but chances are you only know half the story. Make the call. Tap the text. Write the letter. Send the e-mail. Take time for the conversation in the hallway at work.

I'll wrap up this chapter with something fun. Ron Deal's late grandmother, Lorain, had a passion for helping couples thrive in their marriages. For fifty-two years, she crisscrossed the state of Oklahoma with her husband, Homer, as he preached from church to church. Along the way she came up with a succinct formula for marital happiness, whether it's the first, second, or third time. Here's her recipe for a happy marriage:

- 1 cup consideration
- 1 cup courtesy
- 2 cups praise
- 2 cups flattery carefully concealed
- 2 cups milk of human kindness
- 1 gallon faith in God and each other
- 1 small pinch of in-laws
- 1 reasonable budget
- 1 cup contentment

- A generous dash cooperation
- 2 children (at least)
- 1 cup confidence and encouragement (for each)
- 1 large or several small hobbies
- 1 cup blindness to the other's faults

Flavor with frequent portions of recreation and a dash of happy memories. Stir well and remove any specks of jealousy, temper, or criticism. Sweeten well with generous portions of love and keep warm with a steady flame of devotion. Never serve with a cold shoulder or hot tongue.

CHAPTER ELEVEN

Lessons at the End of Life

The bitterest tears shed over graves are for words left unsaid and deeds left undone.[1]

—Harriet Beecher Stowe

On a cold and sunny Rocky Mountain afternoon in February, Jim Downing, a longtime member of the evangelistic organization the Navigators, peers southward out his large bedroom window. In the distance he can see Cheyenne Mountain, once home to the U.S. Space Command and still an active military base. An open Bible rests on a small table before him; an iPhone sits on his nightstand, buzzing with each incoming text message; and there are papers all over the room. He's writing a book and is engaged in a small disagreement with his editor. "They want it to be more of a teaching book," he says. "I want it to be more biographical. I think it needs a little blood and guts. That's what people want."

Jim Downing is 103 and the oldest known survivor of Pearl Harbor. The older he gets, the more attention he seems to receive from news outlets wanting to talk about his recollections of December 7, 1941. He's always happy to oblige, and his memory remains razor sharp. In fact, over the past few years, he's forged a special friendship with a local reporter. He led her to the Lord, and they meet each Tuesday for a Bible study. She calls him "Grandpa Jim," and he considers her his best friend.

"To be honest," Jim says, "although people like to ask me about World War II, I'm not very interested in the past," he says. "And I don't think a lot about the future. Instead, I love to think about today, because today is so much fun!" His friends and colleagues credit that excitement and enthusiasm for his robust constitution. He now needs a motorized chair to get around, but Jim continues to teach and speak each week. "When my wife of sixty-nine years, Morena, died," he says, "my full calendar was a blessing. Even as she began to grow weak, I continued to accept invitations to speak. Just a week after her funeral, I was back teaching. When most people lose a spouse, they think, 'Oh no! What am I going to do?' Well, I knew. I stayed busy."

ENDING WHERE YOU STARTED

Jim and Morena met in October 1939. Jim was a member of the U.S. Navy, stationed in Southern California and already active in the Navigators. Morena was leading a Navigators girls Bible club, and they met at the office of Dawson Trotman, the organization's founder. They were married on July 11, 1941, in Honolulu.

Seventy-five years later, Jim says people often ask him for the secret to a happy marriage. "First," he says, a wry smile creeping across his face, "I always tell them, 'Never question your wife's judgment.' After all, look who she picked out for a husband! But in all seriousness, here is the answer, it's found in 1 Peter 3:2–4. I like the Amplified version." Picking up his Bible, he reads aloud:

> ... when they see your modest and respectful behavior [together with your devotion and appreciation—love your husband, encourage him, and enjoy him as a blessing from God]. Your adornment must not be merely external—with interweaving and elaborate knotting of the hair, and wearing gold jewelry, or [being superficially preoccupied with] dressing in expensive clothes; but let it be [the inner beauty of] the hidden person of the heart, with the imperishable quality and unfading charm of a gentle and peaceful spirit, [one that is calm and self-controlled, not overanxious, but serene and spiritually mature] which is very precious in the sight of God.

Placing the Bible back down on the table, he takes a deep breath and reflects: "A wife must feel secure. A husband must assure her that she's the most important person in the world to him. She must be the center of his universe. And a husband must know that his wife respects him. The only affirmation he needs is her affirmation." Whether it's his years or temperament or both, Jim doesn't overly romanticize the institution of marriage. "Let's face it," he says, matter-of-factly, "women are a lot smarter than men. Man is a very egotistical creature. A wife must understand that and respond accordingly. But I like to say there are three stages to every marriage. The first stage is, 'I can't get along without you.' The second stage is, 'I can't get along with you.' The third and final stage is, 'I can't get along without you.' Happy couples end the way they started."

THE PERSPECTIVE OF TIME

Just a few miles east of Jim Downing's home in Colorado Springs is an assisted living complex, where you'll find men and women in the twilight of their lives. Many are widowed, but others are still married, some after fifty or sixty or more years. What has marriage taught them about love and life? What advice would they give to couples just starting out? If they had to do it all over again, what would they do differently? After all, the passage of time brings perspective. What was so important to us years ago might now seem trivial.

One of these men missed his son's Little League championship game in order to close a big deal. His wife sat alone in the stands, desperate to share with him the golden moment of their only son's childhood. Each time the boy looked up into the bleachers hoping to see his dad, she had to simply shrug. "I spent the money I made on that deal on a car that was eventually totaled," he said. "It was a stupid decision. I wish I could go back and sit with my wife to watch that game."

Matt was a neurosurgeon. He and his wife have been married for sixty-three years. "I had a lot of opportunities to stray while I was a hot-shot doctor," he says, his voice now halting and in a whisper. "But I took my vows seriously. I couldn't do it to Helen." When asked his secret to a long and happy marriage, he said, "Stay busy. That way you won't have any time to fight."

Eleanor, married to her high school sweetheart for forty years, has three suggestions for couples just starting out or well on their way together. "Ladies, respect your husband," she says. "Never cut him down. Never treat him like a child. Never talk bad about him to anybody." Second, she stresses the importance of avoiding a critical spirit. "Always assume your mate has the right motives and is trying to do the right thing." Finally, she suggests that "if you think of that perfect nasty comeback in the heat of an argument, don't say it. You will definitely regret it later. Instead, pray silently for the will to treat your mate with love and respect."

THE CHALLENGES OF BEING UNEQUALLY YOKED

Marie and Bob were married for sixty years. Friends since childhood, they were inseparable until Bob's death from cancer. She misses him terribly but enjoys the peace of knowing her beloved is finally whole and healed. They loved the ocean. "Whenever I see a seagull," Marie reflects, "I think of Bob. I'll be feeling lonely and suddenly look up to see a seagull swoop down into my sight. It's almost as if the Lord is telling me, 'See, everything is going to be all right.'"

But Marie and Bob's marriage had a rocky start. In fact, the first twenty-six years were so difficult that they even considered divorcing. "Bob wasn't a Christian," Marie says. "I knew the Lord loved him. I knew I loved him. We loved each other, but we didn't share the most important things. It caused a lot of tension. Finally, out of desperation, I asked him if he would go to a retreat. He agreed. He came back a completely different man after having accepted Jesus Christ as his personal Lord and Savior." From that point on, their marriage got better and better.

The importance of shared faith in a marriage cannot be overstated. The Apostle Paul was blunt in his admonition to the Christians of Corinth: "Do not be unequally yoked with unbelievers. For what partnership has righteousness with lawlessness? Or what fellowship has light with darkness?" (2 Cor. 6:14, ESV). Those may be hard words for some, but God included them in His Word for a purpose. Pastor John Piper keenly observes, "How can you be intimately, psychologically, spiritually, physically involved with a man who does not say 'Jesus is Lord,' a man who doesn't love your Savior?" Indeed, as Marie suggested, marriage is a union between a man and a woman at every level of life. The effect of not having the most fundamental thing in common will sooner or later be felt, especially after children arrive.

LOOKING BACK, LOOKING AHEAD

In putting this book together, I went back to a Focus on the Family radio broadcast from 1991 that featured couples who had been married for many years. In the intervening quarter century, the voices of all those couples have been silenced, reminding us that life is like "a wind that passes and does not return" (Ps. 78:39, NASB). Every young married couple ought to visit a nursing home. Walk those halls and talk with the residents. You'll find they're not very different from you. They walked the road you're on now, experiencing many if not all of the same challenges, facing the same temptations, and struggling to keep their love alive. These seasoned citizens have answers; we simply have to ask them the right questions.

Calling into that radio program was Beatrice Heron, who gave a moving tribute to Alvin, her husband of sixty years. "He never grumbles," she said, "and he never finds fault with people. He always looks to the good of everyone he sees and tries to pick out something good. Everything I do, he praises me. Maybe the pies don't turn out just right, but just to hear him talk about it, why you'd think they were wonderful. 'That's all right,' he'll say. 'Let's just forget about it. Everything's going to be okay.' We're so thankful that we can live together all these years. I just hope that all the rest of our years will be happy ones, just like the ones that are in the past."

Is it any wonder that Beatrice and Alvin were happily married for so many years? They had their faults like all of us. Yet the Herons had a beautiful marriage because they treated one another with respect. There was an obvious gentleness to Alvin's treatment of Beatrice. In hearing Beatrice, I'm reminded of my own wife's observation: "Treat your husband like a king, and he'll treat you like a queen."

REALISTIC ROMANCE

One of the lessons that longtime married couples commonly cite isn't very romantic. It's what you might call a "live and let live" approach. "I spent the first twenty-five years of my life trying to change Bob," Mary reflected, "and I failed miserably. Our marriage was a constant struggle. I spent the next twenty-five years working to change myself. And our marriage was never better." Jean likes to remind me that you're not supposed to reshape your spouse in your own image but to cooperate with the Holy Spirit as he shapes both of you in the image of Christ. If your spouse needs major changes, that's a job for the Lord and your mate. We can pray for change, but the best thing we can do is concentrate on changing ourselves.

In reflecting on his sixty-nine-year union with Morena, Jim Downing was candid about some of their struggles. "We didn't have as many things in common as some people might think," he said. "Over time we realized that God gave each of us different gifts. The key is to give your spouse enough room to develop them." Jim clearly adored his wife, but he didn't necessarily have to spend every waking minute with her in order to enjoy a fulfilled marriage. A colleague of mine once told me that his mother used to crave her time of solitude and actually liked it when her husband would leave the house. "I didn't mind him leaving," she said, "but it felt good knowing that he was coming back."

Six years after Morena's death, Jim was asked what he missed most about her. It only took him a second to respond: "Her companionship. What I miss now is coming home and having someone to share my excitement with, to talk about the people I met and the new ideas the Lord gave me. Oh, I have children [the Downings had seven] and friends, and I can talk with them, but it's just not the same." A reader of my blog recently shared a similar observation about his widowed mother. "My dad just died a few months ago," he wrote. "I can see now that what my mother probably misses most about my dad is that she is not being cherished by anyone like he did for her—no one to pull the covers over you when you go to bed and just tenderly be there for life together. So take the time to cherish your mate."

SHARED GOALS

Anne and Jimmy Pierson's marriage of fifty-two years was a little different. "We were together 24/7 when we started the House of His Creation, a maternity home in Pennsylvania," wrote Anne. "We were very involved in the beginning of the pro-life movement and had two girls (one was mentally challenged and had multiple handicaps). Our marriage was full of fun, laughter, tears and commitment. He was my best friend, and as we traveled and spoke around the country we would laugh and sing at the top of our voices in the car. When I first met him he told me more than anything he wanted to be a father. He said he would work hard, but being a father was first. He got his dream and so did I." The Piersons would go on to assist over two hundred women and their babies. Anne and Jimmy had a dream. They committed it to the Lord in prayer, and the Lord answered it many times over.

"A STRANGER IN HER MIND"

Howard Coville, eighty-four years old when he called our radio program back in 1991, lived in a retirement home with his wife, who had Alzheimer's disease. "Sometimes she knows me and sometimes she doesn't," he said. "She may be confused as to who I am, but she knows that it's somebody that loves her and who she loves. Usually when I see her, we'll cry together for a minute or two, and then she'll kind of quiet down, and I just tell her I love her. Our love is very real and vital, and we're so thankful to our Lord for it all. I can't walk too much anymore, and I'm getting old, but my love stays young for my wife. My love remains young because, at heart, it is young. She's my lifelong lover; she's my girl."

While culling the wisdom of our most seasoned believers, I came across many people facing Alzheimer's or some form of dementia. We all know somebody in that difficult position, and each story is heartbreaking. A songwriter named Mark "Brink" Brinkman penned a moving ballad, "She's a Stranger in His Mind," written from the perspective of a woman whose husband can no longer remember her.[2] Brinkman's lyrics describe a profoundly sad situation, one that he calls "unkind." And it is good to be reminded that yes, life *can* be unkind. The sooner a couple can come to terms with the reality that difficulty is part of every marriage, the easier it will be for husbands and wives to weather the storms of life. I have observed that couples who weather misfortune eventually enjoy a special sweetness, especially in the later years of marriage. The rivalries and jealousies of youth have faded, they've grown comfortable in their own skin, they know what they like and what they don't. The game playing is over; they're no longer keeping score. More important, they know what their spouses like or will tolerate, and their goal is to serve them rather than themselves.

CHAPTER TWELVE

More Secrets to a Great Marriage

For a married couple to expect perfection in each other is unrealistic. The unblemished idea exists only in "happily ever after" fairy tales. I think there is merit to a description I once read of a married couple as "happily incompatible."[1]

—Dr. Billy Graham

What's the best piece of marriage advice you've ever received? I have been thinking back across the years and pondering that very question. In three decades of marriage, I've read lots of books on the subject, participated in Bible studies, and contributed to dozens of marriage projects. I've been to many weddings and have heard wonderful sermons on the topic. In addition, I've had the privilege of devoting the past twenty-five years to a ministry dedicated to helping couples forge biblically centered unions. I'm surrounded by counselors and family psychologists. And since 2010, I've hosted more than two thousand radio programs, many of which have featured the country's leading Christian marriage experts.

It is difficult, then, to boil down all the wisdom I've received to just one or two adages, but I'm going to try. The first "best piece of advice" I've received actually came to me before Jean and I were married. We had enrolled in a premarital counseling program, a wise decision that I would strongly encourage all engaged couples to make. The instructor reminded us that for Christians, divorce is not an option. Or as a friend of mine would say, "When it comes to your marriage, there is no plan B." The sacredness of the institution demands that when troubles come, as they surely will, divorce is not on the table.

This simple piece of advice saved our marriage when it was just getting started. When Jean first revealed her struggle with depression, she told me, "You deserve someone who is stronger than I am. You can do better than me." I vehemently disagreed, assuring her that I loved her and was committed to her for the rest of my life. "If you're leaving me," I told her, "I'm going with you." Where did that rock-solid decisiveness come from? The answer is obvious. I had made an ironclad commitment from the very beginning of our marriage that divorce was not an option.

The second "best piece of advice" that transformed our marriage might strike some of you as a bit silly, but it's made a big difference in how I express my frustrations or challenges with Jean. "Whenever you're in an argument," a friend once told me, "imagine that Jesus is standing just over your wife's shoulder." In other words, I know that anything I say to Jean, I'm also saying to the Lord. This adjustment radically changes my choice of words when working through a tough conversation. Am I addressing Jean with words of honor, or am I being overly critical and condemning? Am I being respectful? Would I be embarrassed to see my words in print? We often underestimate the effect our words can have, for good or ill, on our spouse. "Death and life are in the power of the tongue," says Solomon, "and those who love it will eat its fruits" (Prov. 18:21, ESV).

ADVICE FROM THE WORLD'S LONGEST-MARRIED COUPLES

Although fewer couples are choosing to marry at all, according to the U.S. Census Bureau, more couples are remaining married than in years past. For example, since 1990, 77 percent of couples have reached their tenth anniversaries, up from 74 percent in the 1980s.[2] Fifty-five percent of married couples have been together for at least fifteen years, and 35 percent have reached the quarter-century mark. Just 6 percent of couples in the United States make it or have made it to their golden anniversary, though death, not divorce, accounts for that low statistic.[3]

But what about those rare few who make it past five decades? Is there something we can learn from them? I believe so. As I write, Karam and Kartari Chand of Great Britain are the world's longest-married couple, having celebrated their ninetieth wedding anniversary in December 2015.[4] Karam, 110, and Kartari, a spry 103, have eight children, twenty-seven grandchildren, and twenty-three great-grandchildren.

The secret to their longevity may be that they don't believe in eating anything artificial. As for their marital happiness, they subscribe to a threefold formula. First, they advocate keeping no secrets from one another. Second, they try not to argue. And third, they spend each day surrounded by family, a practice that's a challenge in Western society, where generations rarely live together. "We have not spent any long span apart in more than fifty years," says Karam. "We go everywhere together—up until a few years ago we went to India every year with the family, and for all family weddings we make sure we get to stay together."[5] But he really comes alive when the subject turns to humor. "My trick is to make Kartari laugh. I like to tell jokes and make her smile. Being funny is my way of being romantic. I have been told laughing makes you live longer—my wife is still alive, so it must have worked. I love her, and I want to spend another eighty years by her side."[6] Karam is my kind of guy!

In the Far East, Zhang Mucheng and Xu Dongying of China celebrated their eighty-sixth anniversary in 2015. It was an arranged marriage, Zhang recalls, rather unromantically: "At that time we didn't have many choices. All you could do was hope to find a good girl who could help you with housecleaning."[7] The couple has eight children—five sons and three daughters. "We just feel good when we are together," says Xu. When asked their secret to a long and happy marriage, Zhang replies, "Our relationship philosophy is, 'To lose is to gain.'...If you're unhappy about something, don't dwell on it. Try to understand each other's point of view, give in to one another and forgive each other." Xu also stresses the value of shared interests. "We have so many things to do together. We don't have time for fights."[8]

Closer to home, John and Anna Betar held the distinction of being America's longest-married couple when they celebrated their eighty-third anniversary,[9] though their wedding almost never happened. Anna's father tried to convince her to marry another man, who was twenty years older. She resisted, and the rest is history. The Betars' advice? "Don't hold a grudge. Forgive each other. Live accordingly," says John. Anna agrees, noting, "We are very fortunate. It is unconditional love and understanding. We have had that. We consider it a blessing."[10]

SNAPSHOTS OF LOVE

Lauren Fleishman, a photographer, set out to capture images of longtime romance after finding her late grandfather's love letters stashed away in a drawer. The discovery cast Joseph Kalish's fifty-nine-year marriage to Doris in a new light, reminding Lauren that he wasn't always the old man she knew. She traveled throughout the United States and across Europe to photograph and interview couples together for fifty years or more. "I wasn't looking at them in terms of their age," she says. "I was looking at them in terms of their love. They're not really photographs of old people. They're photographs of people in love."[11] The six-year odyssey, which resulted in the publication of *The Lovers*,[12] took her from senior dances to retirement homes. What common themes did the thirty-five-year-old Fleishman see emerge from all her subjects? "I think the thing that I've learned is that love seems to get deeper as you go along," she said, adding, "They all had their fair share of compromises. None of them say it's been a smooth road."[13]

Fred and Frances Futterman, two of Fleishman's subjects, have been married for sixty-eight years. "As you grow older, love changes," they observe. "It changes because we change."[14] Joseph and Dorothy Bolotin have been married for seventy-eight years. But according to Dorothy, "I never think of it in terms of years. I think of it in terms of good years. In love, hot romance doesn't last forever. So I would say that, yes, I think love changes. I would say we're still in love. We still love each other. It's focusing, doing little things. He's an amazing man."[15]

Sheila and David Newman were married in 1957. They believe it's critical to support each other's pursuits. "David always supported any interests I had," reflects Sheila. "He supported me with whatever I did, told me I should do the best I can. And I was anti-intellectual when I married him. I got to love music because he practiced a lot and I listened to him—he explained everything. We really changed, we enriched each other's lives."[16]

Fleishman captured Yaakov and Mariya Shapirshteyn of Brooklyn on the beach just prior to their daily summer swim. Clad only in a gray Speedo, Yaakov says with a smile, "What is the secret to love? A secret is a secret. I'm seventy-five and I don't reveal my secrets."[17]

TRANSFORMING INSIGHTS

Marriage may not be easy, but at least there's plenty of good advice available. A few years ago, I collected a bookful of it in *The Best Advice I Ever Got on Marriage*,[18] and I'd like to share some of my favorite passages from that project. My colleague Dr. Greg Smalley wrote, "The greatest marriage advice I've ever heard came from one of the most unlikely places"—a Kay Jewelers advertising slogan: "If your heart is open, love will always find a way in."[19] Greg goes on to emphasize that an open heart is "the fundamental prerequisite for a great marriage." I couldn't agree more. When your heart is cold and closing down, there's little room for the Lord to work.

Andy Stanley, the founder of North Point Ministries, a bestselling author, and father of two sons and a daughter, offers blunt and straightforward advice:

> If you want to go deep, if you want real intimacy, then you live as if your loved one is more important than you—which means his or her interests become at least as important as yours. Besides sharing their interests, how do you treat those who are more important than you? Let me tell you: you defer to them. You don't interrupt and say, "No, no. I think that was blue, not red." You don't pat them on the back and say, "Posture, posture." You laugh even when they're not funny. The key is respect, respect, respect. Through your actions, through what you say, through what you don't say, through the way you say it, you respect them and treat them as if they are more important than you.[20]

The advice I got about imagining our Savior standing beside your spouse goes to the same point. It is absolutely critical that your interactions with your wife or husband be loving, gracious, and polite. There is no place for rudeness or thoughtlessness.

In a similar vein, Gary Thomas, the bestselling author of *The Sacred Marriage*, recommends seeing God as your father-in-law, since your spouse is His child:

> When I realized I am married to God's daughter—and that you, women, are married to God's sons—my view of marriage completely changed. God feels about my wife—His daughter—in an even holier and more passionate way than I feel about my own daughters. Suddenly, my marriage was no longer about just me and one other person; it was very much a relationship with a passionately interested third Partner as well. In fact, I realized that one of my primary forms of worship throughout the rest of my life would be honoring God by taking care of a woman who would always be, in His divine mind, "His little girl."[21]

We might joke about our in-laws, but it's no laughing matter to keep in mind that our spouse is loved by his or her Heavenly Father and that if we want to honor Him, we must honor His child.

Ted Cunningham, the pastor of Woodland Hills Family Church in Branson, Missouri, stresses the importance of having a good time together—laughing and telling jokes, pursuing leisure and adventure activities, and relaxing together on the back porch or by the pool. We shouldn't view our marriage as just another task on our to-do list:

> You can enjoy life with your spouse in the midst of the grind: "Enjoy life with your wife, whom you love, all the days of this meaningless life that God has given you under the sun—all your meaningless days. For this is your lot in life and in your toilsome labor under the sun" (Ecclesiastes 9:9). Laugh in the midst of the grind, and remember not to take yourself too seriously. Proverbs 17:22 says, "A cheerful heart is good medicine." Your marriage needs several good doses of this medicine. Don't keep it hidden away and stored in the medicine cabinet. Thank you, Lord,

> for the gift of laughter. Now go! Enjoy life with your spouse.[22]

Are you enjoying your spouse? Or has your marriage become just another part of the grind? Perhaps it's time to shake things up. Rent a comedy on Netflix, go see a show. Or maybe even just reminisce. Jean and I enjoy laughing about our honeymoon in Mexico. We arrived with such great expectations, but within hours I fell ill with fever, chills, and nausea. Jean soon followed. The entire week was a washout. Here we were on our honeymoon, and I couldn't even touch her! So go ahead and laugh. As Bob Hope once said, laughter is an "instant vacation." Our family can attest to that. We love to laugh together. It binds us together and enables joy, love, and grace to flourish in our home. Simply put, laughter makes our house a pleasant place to be. The climate is always better in our home when Jean's laughing. The more we laugh, the more we *enjoy* one another's company, and that strengthens our relationships. That experience isn't unique to us.

Did you know that the more family members laugh together, the less likely they are to experience depression or to be overcome by stress? To be sure, life offers plenty of genuine trouble that is no laughing matter. But sometimes it's easy to make mountains out of molehills. When couples can laugh at the routine ups and downs of life, they're better equipped to feel compassion for others in the midst of *their* struggles. Perhaps that's what the essayist Agnes Repplier meant when she said, "We cannot really love anybody with whom we never laugh."

ADVICE FROM THE TRENCHES

Some of the best marriage advice you'll find anywhere comes not from the "experts" but from an abundant source of experience, fidelity, and wisdom that I encounter every day—the friends and listeners of the Focus on the Family radio program. The following tips should give any husband or wife plenty to work on:

Do your duty to your wife as unto the Lord—as if your wife were perfect. It doesn't matter if she messes up or offends you; you still have to do the right thing.

Be kind to each other. Sounds simple but…

Never go to bed angry.

God gave you two ears and one mouth. Listen!

The majority of marital problems can be boiled down to one word: selfishness.

Be careful what you say, because you can never take words back once they've been said.

My Aunt Mildred, who lived to be 101, said if she could have done things over again, the one change she would have made was to put her husband first. She felt that she had put her children first and that if she had put her husband first instead, their life would have been so much better.

Marriage requires each party to give 100 percent. Only divorce is 50/50.

Marriage is not so much finding the right person as being the right person.

Before you have an argument, ask yourself, "Is this the hill I want to die on?"

Don't sweat the small stuff. And it's all small stuff.

Be a student of your spouse. What motivates him or her? What makes him or her happy, sad, frustrated, excited, inspired? What discourages him or her? Discover everything about him or her you possibly can.

I asked my friend why her marriage ended. She said, "He would treat a stranger on the street with more joy and respect than he would me." I vowed that day that my husband would get more joy and more respect than anyone else did from me. He deserves the first fruits, not the scraps.

Talk to and treat your spouse the way you want to be talked to and treated.

Don't forget to laugh and have fun.

Never make your spouse the butt of your jokes.

Marry someone who is different from you.

The centerpiece of Mom's and Dad's sixty-five-year marriage was to "give and forgive."

Give your spouse the benefit of the doubt.

Your spouse is on your side. You're partners, not enemies.

Try to not speak in anger. Cool down, collect yourself, and then discuss. Speak when it is wise to do so.

Marry someone who has your same faith and worldview. Jesus is the rock!

Serve each other.

Dream about the future together.

Have kids! Children are the joy of a home, and they unite you in common purpose.

It's a marathon, not a sprint!

Avoid using the words "always" and "never."

If you float, your relationship will decay. You have to swim upstream every day. Make small corrections early and often. If you sense it, talk about it.

Always look for a third alternative when problem-solving. It doesn't always have to be his way or her way. There may be an even better alternative.

Presume the best.

Treat each other as if today were the first day of your marriage.

Have coffee and talk on the back porch Saturday mornings before the kids get up.

You can never communicate too much. My husband and I practically have daily meetings, and while it sounds a bit corporate, it has helped us so much. If you fully understand your partner's perspective (you don't necessarily have to agree), you will be much better prepared when something big and bad happens.

Gary Thomas once wrote that most get married "to be loved," but in marriage God teaches us "how to love."

Always try to act as you want to feel, even if you're not feeling it.

Always be willing to say you are sorry.

Covenant eyes. Don't stalk or befriend an ex on Facebook.

Don't trash talk your spouse with friends.

Smile until you mean it.

If your spouse were just like you, you would be bored and God would not have the opportunity to make you more like Jesus.

Spend the first thirty minutes of each day together (no cellphones).

Don't nit-pick.

Humility counts for so much. You will never have a thoroughly authentic relationship with your spouse, with God, a friend, or your child if the Lord is forbidden from speaking to the deepest wounds and sins you face. Fear and pride will block the ability to get there.

Since my husband is my favorite person, I decided that I would try always to behave in a way that makes me his favorite person. Not constantly going above and beyond to try to impress him, but to act and react in a way that's kind. So that in times when we disagree, he doesn't think of me in a disagreeable way. I try to listen to myself speak and ask myself if I would mind being talked to that way.

Be honest, loyal, and grateful.

Date night every week and one weekend away together every year.

Stop fighting each other and start fighting the enemy—Satan.

Pray individually, pray together, pray for each other.

Seek Christ and happiness will be in Him. Marriage is more about being holy than happy.

Make two commitments to stay married: the first on your wedding day ("till death do us part") and the second on every day that follows. The day you take it for granted is the day the commitment begins to falter.

Don't think of any chores as women's or men's. The more you help each other, the more time you have to do other things and enjoy each other.

I can't change my spouse. If I want things to change in my marriage, I have to change myself—my attitudes, my words, my actions.

Don't bring your marital problems to your parents.

Get to know your spouse's family really well. Don't assume you know them, but take time and observe.

Children will feel the most secure if their parents' marriage is secure, so put the marriage in the front seat, kids in the backseat. Parents of toddlers must remind themselves of this all the time.

Set boundaries so others (friends, family, work, etc.) will not smother your marriage.

Hang in there. The first one hundred years are the hardest.

Be the first one to say "I'm sorry!"

The grass is greener where you water it.

The best gift you can give your children is to love your spouse.

Jesus comes first. Your spouse comes second. You come last.

How's that for a list? If you have anything to add, I invite you to e-mail me at Focus on the Family.

By now you've realized that your spouse is unlike anyone else in the world. Do you treasure him or her as the unique creation he or she is? Marriage is wonderful and challenging. It's difficult, sacred, and fragile. But it should also be filled with joy and fun. Are you willing to put in the work to make your marriage the best it can be? I pray so.

STANDING FIRM IN OBEDIENCE TO CHRIST

We tend to think that the times we live in are more difficult than earlier times, that it's more difficult to stay happily married today than it was fifty years ago. I don't believe it is. Yes, these are strange and even unsettling times, but we have an opportunity to let our light shine more brightly in the darkness.

Several years ago, I added my signature to a powerful statement—"The Two Shall Become One Flesh: Reclaiming Marriage"[23]—published by Evangelicals and Catholics Together, a group founded by one of my heroes, Chuck Colson, and the extraordinary Father Richard John Neuhaus. Both men have completed their earthly journeys, but their commitment to the sacredness of the institution of marriage continues to inspire. They never grew tired of posing powerful arguments for the truth and beauty of God's design for marriage. And neither should we. This exhortation should be a charge to all of us as followers of Christ:

> All Christians and men and women of good will must work to rebuild the culture of marriage and live lives that attest to the joy and beauty of marriage.... Keeping in mind the obligation to speak the truth in love, we must find ways to distinguish true marriage from its distortion, and we must do so without abandoning the public square. We owe our fellow citizens a socially engaged witness to the truth about marriage, which, with the family, is the unalterable foundation of a healthy, humane society.
>
> The time is approaching—indeed, in some instances it has already arrived—when Christians in this country will

> suffer abuse for upholding the truth about marriage. We encourage our fellow Christians to stand firm in obedience to Christ, for that obedience is the most compassionate service we can offer society. In doing so, we must strive to heal the wounds of a confused and broken culture, to foster human flourishing, and to honor the God who created human beings in His own image, male and female. For Christ said, "I came that they may have life, and have it abundantly" (John 10:10).

Amen and amen!

PART III

The Twelve Traits of Highly Successful Marriages

Your Personalized Marriage Assessment

What are the strengths and weaknesses in your marriage? Would you like to find out? You're in the right place. My colleague Dr. Greg Smalley and his wife, Erin, have studied thousands of strong couples across the country and identified twelve essential traits of successful marriages. The traits are both biblically based and practical. You can learn more in the Smalleys' wonderful new book, *Crazy Little Thing Called Marriage: 12 Secrets of Lifelong Romance.*[1]

But for now, I invite you to go online and get your own free marriage assessment: www.focusonthefamily.com/marriagedoneright.

You and your spouse should complete the questionnaire separately. It takes only about ten minutes. After you get your results, come back to this section of the book and work your way through the following studies for each of the twelve traits of successful marriages, including the discussion questions that will guide you in a conversation with your spouse.

TRAIT 1

Cherish

Can a mother forget the baby at her breast and have no compassion on the child she has borne? Though she may forget, I will not forget you! See, I have engraved you on the palms of my hands. . . .

—Isaiah 49:15–16, NIV

Couples who cherish one another recognize that each spouse is created in God's image and is therefore of infinite worth. They understand that God made everyone different, and so they treasure each other's unique characteristics. Thriving couples work to keep an attitude of respect and appreciation for each other (Phil. 2:3). They remember what they value about their marriage, keep reminders of good memories, and celebrate milestones together.

Worth. Treasure. Love. Tenderness. These are just a few of the words that might describe the act of cherishing. However you describe it, it is integral to the harmony and stability of a marriage and a family. It's important to add that your spouse can't *earn* this kind of worth. It's a gift you give unconditionally.

Your wedding vows probably included a promise "to love and to cherish" one another. Do you think you have lived up to those vows? If not, here are a few things you can do to start beefing up the cherishing aspect of your relationship.

1. Treasuring

The Apostle Paul tells us that a Christian is like an old clay pot. On the outside the pot is dull and unremarkable. But it contains an indescribable treasure—the treasure of Christ's eternal glory (2 Cor. 4:7).

Whether you realize it or not, you are living every day of your life in the presence of a precious hidden treasure. It sits with you at the table and sleeps beside you in bed at night. It's so close that you can reach out and touch it any time you like. It's the treasure that lies concealed within the person you chose to marry.

Unfortunately, time has a way of tarnishing the treasure, making it appear plain and mundane. When this happens, husbands and wives lose sight of the hidden mystery that drew them together in the first place. And that's tragic, because treasure is all about mystery. "Treasure" is the word we use to describe things that are not merely valuable in monetary terms but deeply significant—things like the Holy Grail or the Ark of the Covenant.

Marriage partners need to keep this sense of significance alive at the heart of their relationship. They need to learn how to treasure and cherish one another by intentionally lifting their old feelings of attraction and romance out of the realm of mere emotion and transforming them into a steady, consistent attitude.

2. Remembering

Exactly how is this "treasuring" accomplished? The answer is simple: by *remembering*. When life becomes comfortable, familiar, and routine, most of us get complacent. We forget the blessings we've received. That's why God so often had to remind the people of Israel of the many wonders He had performed on their behalf (Isa. 46:9).

That's why Jesus established the Lord's Supper as a memorial of His redeeming work on the cross (Luke 22:19).

If you and your spouse have lost sight of the sparkle that led you to the altar, it's time to reach back into your shared past and reclaim it. Once it's within your grasp, it's a good idea to keep going—try to remember all the little incidents along the pathway of marriage that have made you precious to one another. Memory is a powerful tool. If you want a strong marriage, you have to know how to make the most of it.

3. Keeping a record

Greg Smalley describes how he once found his father, the marriage expert and counselor Gary Smalley, staring intently at his computer screen. "What are you looking at?" asked Greg. "Well," his dad began, "a number of years ago I started a list of why your mom is so valuable. So when I'm upset with her or when we've had a fight, instead of sitting here thinking about how hurt or frustrated I am, I make myself read through this list."

Gary had laid hold of a vital truth. Thriving couples intentionally treasure and honor one another by keeping a conscious account of the things they value about their relationship. Just as God's people would set up "stones of remembrance" to commemorate the Lord's mighty works, you can preserve precious memories and reminders of ongoing blessings in a tangible form—for example, by keeping a journal or writing down a list of the qualities you love and admire most in your spouse (and sharing it with him or her as opportunities arise). It's also important to take time out to celebrate anniversaries and other marital milestones. These occasions can be enhanced by special gifts—for example, a ring or a pendant—to commemorate important events in your life as a couple.

4. Looking ahead

You can bring cherishing to an even higher level by finding ways not only to keep in touch with the past but to project the past into the future.

Putting It into Practice

God's Word is living, active, and powerful (Heb. 4:12), and our relationship with the Lord must be as well. The wonders He performed yesterday mean nothing unless they inspire and guide us today and tomorrow.

It's the same in marriage. The cherishing at the heart of the marital union must be a living thing. Sometimes when a couple's relationship begins to falter, they try to restore it by recapturing the feelings they had for one another back in the "good old days." That's fine, but it isn't enough to propel their marriage forward into the next phase. If you want to grow in your ability to love and honor one another, you have to turn yesterday's good times into a springboard to the great things God has in store up ahead.

Questions for Discussion

1. How can we be more intentional about rediscovering, cherishing, and celebrating the hidden and mysterious treasures we recognize in one another? How can we prevent routine from breeding boredom in the life we share?
2. How can we keep the thread of God's plan for our lives unbroken as we move together from the past into the future?
3. What is one way I can let you know that I *cherish* you over the coming week?

TRAIT 2

Lifelong Commitment

But Ruth said, "Do not urge me to leave you or to return from following you. For where you go I will go, and where you lodge I will lodge. Your people shall be my people, and your God my God. Where you die I will die, and there will I be buried. May the Lord do so to me and more also if anything but death parts me from you."

—Ruth 1:16–17, ESV

What does it mean when a person says, "I am committed to my marriage for life"?

It means, among other things, that marriage is *established by God* and meant to be *honored* by everyone (Heb. 13:4). Healthy couples believe marriage is *permanent* and that divorce is not an option. They look forward to their future together and see their marriage as one of the most important parts of their lives. They love each other and invest in their relationship. In strong marriages, couples expect to face challenges together and are willing to do whatever it takes to make their marriage work. How does all this play out in everyday life? Let's take a closer look.

1. Marriage is a priceless gift

Lifelong commitment grows out of a realization that God established marriage and gave it to men and women as a priceless gift. The prophet Malachi says, "God, not you, made marriage. His Spirit inhabits even the smallest details of marriage... so guard the spirit of marriage within you" (2:15, MSG).

Couples who stick together over the long haul understand that marriage is not merely a contractual partnership or a sexual liaison. It's a sacred and solemn spiritual *mystery* in the eyes of God. Of all the human relationships we could name, it's the one used most frequently by the biblical writers to represent Yahweh's covenant with His people and Christ's relationship with the Church (see Eph. 5:31–32; Rev. 21:2).

2. Love is a decision

Lifelong commitment also implies that you love your spouse and make a decision to stay married "till death do us part." In other words, divorce is not an option in your mind. At some point a husband and wife need to *decide* to love—even when they don't feel like it. The Latin root of "decide" means "to cut." You cannot make a commitment without deciding to cut off other options that compete against what is most important.

Burn the ships! In 1519, the conquistador Hernando Cortés landed in Mexico intent on claiming the treasures of the Aztecs. Facing fearsome odds, he burned his ships. With no way out and no way back, his men had no place to go except forward. Successful married couples "burn their ships" by taking the word "divorce" completely out of their vocabulary. It's a simple matter of commitment. "Therefore what God has joined together, let no one separate" (Matt. 19:6, NIV). Remember, retreat is easy when you have the option.

3. You like your marriage relationship

Another aspect of lifelong commitment is the ability to say, "I really like this relationship and want it to continue."

"Marriage should be honored by all. . . ." (Heb. 13:4, NIV). Making the decision to stay together is one way to honor your marriage. But honor and commitment also involve the emotions and feelings. If you can say, "I *value* and *like* this marriage," and really mean it, you're on the road to building a relationship that will go the distance.

4. You take action

Last but not least, commitment isn't simply a matter of deciding to stay married (the will) or liking the relationship (feelings). On the contrary, commitment is primarily about taking active steps to maintain your marriage. As the Bible says, "So also faith by itself, if it does not have works, is dead" (James 2:17, ESV). It's the same way in personal relationships. You demonstrate how important your marriage is to you by investing time and money to make it better. During difficult seasons, you fight for your marriage. In season and out of season, you show yourself willing to do whatever it takes to keep your relationship strong.

Putting It into Practice

Research shows a marriage commitment yields a more satisfying relationship on all levels. Women respond when they know their husbands are willing to "die to self" for them. Men hesitate to invest unless they know there's a payoff. One researcher concluded that "a man tends to give most completely to a woman once he has decided *she is my future.*"

How do you make these concepts real and practical in everyday life? There are a number of ways you can start working toward that goal. You might begin by trying a date night activity that highlights the excitement and adventure of mutual commitment. Come up with some activity that simply won't work unless the two of you decide right up front that you're both going to stick it out to the very end. Dancing naturally comes to mind—after all, it takes two to tango—but there are other sports and activities—tennis, rowing, or an art project, for instance—that might work equally well.

Questions for Discussion

1. What brought us together in the first place? What attracted us to one another? How can we reignite that attraction?

2. What was our *vision* for our marriage when we were just starting out? Where did we see ourselves going together? How can we recapture those original dreams and reaffirm our hopes for a shared future?
3. What were the vows we spoke to one another at our wedding? Why did we make those vows, and how well are we keeping them? Has anything happened to change our commitment to pursuing those goals? If so, what can we do about it? How can we renew and reaffirm our vows to one another at this point in our relationship?

TRAIT 3

Positive Communication

For now we see in a mirror, dimly, but then face to face. Now I know in part, but then I shall know just as I also am known.

—John 16:33, NLT

Positive communication allows couples to become emotionally connected. Two individuals can understand each other better when they listen well and express their needs, thoughts, and feelings honestly. Healthy couples communicate about daily matters, sharing their joys and sorrows, learning more about each other, and their conversations enrich their relationship.

The marriage-triage experts at Focus on the Family's Hope Restored tell us that lack of communication is the most commonly mentioned problem among couples who are struggling to keep their relationships alive. Likewise, the best research indicates that healthy marriages are *always* built around a solid core of open, honest, and empathetic dialogue. It's all about both partners becoming transparent enough to know and be known at the most basic level of their humanity.

How do you foster this kind of dialogue and interaction in a marriage? Here are some ideas to keep in mind.

1. *Vive la différence!*

Men and women are made for community, to be known intimately, to feel understood and desired. Marriage, among all human relationships, is the place where this communion and "in-othering" take place at the deepest and most intimate level. Unfortunately, it doesn't always come easy. As a matter of fact, it can sometimes be the most difficult work you've ever faced.

You and your spouse are different people from different backgrounds. You're also male and female—representatives of the two "halves" of humanity, two *opposite* sexes (Gen. 1:27). You can't read each other's minds. In fact, it's difficult even to relate to each other's viewpoints. This may sound like a problem, but it's actually a blessing. Perhaps you can't peer directly into your spouse's soul, but you can learn to know and to be known intimately, which is better than mind-reading because it forces you to become better marriage partners and better people.

Whatever your differences, you need to do more than grudgingly accept them. You need to rejoice in them, celebrating the lights, darks, and contrasting colors that make up the blended one-flesh union you call "us." Positive communication makes this possible.

2. Enjoy the journey

Thriving couples know that the way they *respond* to their differences is far more important than how they *resolve* them. To state this in broader terms, they understand that, in marriage, it's the process that counts. Real communication is a journey—it's about walking humbly with one another and with God (Mic. 6:8). And the journey is more important than the destination.

Dr. Bob Paul and Dr. Bob Burbee, two of Hope Restored's highly skilled therapists, call this journey "heart talk." People in a close relationship, they explain, actually engage in two types of communication: "work talk" and "heart talk." Work talk is task oriented. It focuses on solving problems and accomplishing goals. Heart talk, on the other hand, tries to go deeper. It's concerned with the relationship and driven by feelings and a desire for understanding. Instead of a task or a goal, it aims at cohesion, attachment, and the strengthening of the interpersonal bond.

How do you do heart talk? It's primarily a matter of caring about the other person's feelings and taking turns as speaker and listener. The people at Hope Restored sum it up with the acronym ICU: *identify* your feelings and the feelings of your spouse, decide to *care* about those feelings, and seek to *understand* those feelings with the assistance of your mate. Then keep on talking and listening until both of you are satisfied with the results.

3. More than words

What keeps so many husbands and wives from experiencing this kind of heart-to-heart connection? Gary Smalley suggests that somewhere along the line they've bought into the idea that real communication occurs when they understand one another's *words*. That's unfortunate, because, as the concept of heart talk demonstrates, words are just the beginning. Genuine two-in-one bonding happens only when we get behind mere verbiage to the heart of the matter.

Interpersonal communication is far more robust and active than mere talk. It requires openness and empathy—a willingness to enter into the thoughts and feelings of another, to weep when he or she weeps and to laugh when he or she laughs. That's because real communication is about knowing and being known from the inside out—and "who among men knows the thoughts of a man except the spirit of the man which is in him?" (1 Cor. 2:11, NASB).

4. Stay curious

Finally, it's important to remember that relationships are dynamic. They change over time, as do the persons in them. There are a couple of reasons for this. On the one hand, people are made in the image of God, which suggests that they are, in a sense, endlessly complex and mysterious. On the other hand, people are finite, mortal, imperfect, and sinful, and this implies that there is always room for growth and improvement in every human personality. No matter how long you are married, then, you will never grasp everything there is to know about your spouse. This is why it's so important to stay curious.

Putting It into Practice

Husbands and wives who stick together are good students of one another. They learn to ask questions instead of passing judgment. Rather than lashing out in anger when a spouse behaves inexplicably, they know how to say, "Tell me what you're thinking" or "Help me understand why you reacted that way in that situation." These couples feel an openness to share with one another on a heart-to-heart level. Not only are they comfortable talking about both facts and feelings, they prioritize communication and schedule regular time to connect, fanning the flames of ongoing romance and keeping the wonder of their first love alive.

Questions for Discussion

1. What practical steps can we take to foster more heart talk in our marriage? How can we become more intentional about resolving the problems of everyday life by means of ICU?

2. What practical steps can we take to stay current with one another? What does it mean to you to be a "student" of me? How can I become a better "student" of you?
3. What does the Bible mean when it says that "Everyone should be quick to listen, slow to speak, and slow to become angry" (James 1:19, NIV)? What can we do to place the principles expressed in this verse more solidly at the center of our relationship?

TRAIT 4

Community-Minded

For as we have many members in one body, but all the members do not have the same function, so we, being many, are one body in Christ, and individually members of one another.

—Romans 12:4–5, NKJV

It takes a community to sustain a marriage. Thriving couples spend time with people who want to see their marriage succeed, and they have good models of marriage in their lives. They have people they can count on in times of need and are careful not to isolate themselves. They choose to interact with those around them for their own good and for the good of others.

Every healthy community is marked by fellowship. In the Bible, "fellowship" connotes a shared vision, community, intimacy, and joint participation. The God of this universe created us to be in relationships with Him and with others. We were never meant to tackle the challenges of life and marriage alone. Couples need a strong community surrounding them at all times.

When you're caught up in the first flush of romantic love, it's easy to adopt a "you and me against the world" attitude. But where do you turn for help when it becomes "you and me against each other"? And what can you do to help when you see other couples falling into the same ditch? The answers can be found in fellowship. Here are a few thoughts on the need for community and some of the best places to find it.

1. The challenge

Let's face it. Marriage can be difficult. Satanic forces more powerful than any comic book archvillain are out to break up every couple's marital commitment (1 Pet. 5:8). And each partner's innate self-centeredness is bound to create problems in a marriage. Even the healthiest relationships go through conflict, disappointment, and temptation. This suggests that family and friends have a continuing role to play in a couple's grand adventure. When hard times come, loved ones who have vowed to support and fight for your marriage can make a life-or-death difference in your relationship. In the same way, you can step in and help rescue others from the marital snares and pitfalls you've successfully survived. It's all a matter of being connected, available, and involved *before* problems arise.

2. The church

The first and most obvious place to make these connections is your local church. We are "members of one another," writes Paul in Romans 12:5 (NKJV). That's the meaning of the Church in a nutshell. Naturally, this is a two-way street: you as a couple need the Church, and the Church needs you. To be strong, you have to learn how to give and to take. God's Word directs all of us to "consider how we may spur one another on toward love and good deeds. Let us not give up meeting together, as some are in the habit of doing, but let us encourage one another" (Heb. 10:24–25, NIV). Married couples are an integral part of the church community.

Remember, Jesus Christ came into the world to become one of us, healing us of our sins, creating us anew, and making us part of a new humanity. There's no place, then, for "me and God" theology in the Christian community. To truly live, we have to step outside our private lives, reach out to our neighbors, and do something for and with other people.

3. Mentoring relationships

Within the larger fellowship of the church, there's a great deal you can do to establish bonds with people on a smaller and more personal level. For example, you can connect regularly with like-minded couples by joining a Sunday school class, Bible study, or fellowship group for married people in your age range.

You can also make yourselves available to mentor newlyweds and younger couples who might benefit from your experience. Like the Apostle Paul in the early Church, you can provide insight, wisdom, and inspiration. All you have to do is be yourselves. Offer an example of an intimate spiritual relationship, of how to work together, of how to be caring, effective parents. You'd be surprised what *you* can gain by offering empathy and encouragement to husbands and wives whose marriages are in need of practical, tangible assistance. As in the life of the Church at large, a mentoring relationship is very much a two-way street.

4. Community outreach

Thriving couples who desire to bear witness for Christ in the world look beyond the walls of the church, interacting with both believers and nonbelievers in their neighborhoods and local communities. They engage with nurturing groups of all kinds—service organizations, social clubs, and common-interest groups. This kind of involvement is crucial to the health of your marriage and a strong indicator of its vitality. The strength of the bond that holds you and your spouse together is directly related to the value you place on human relationships of every variety.

Wondering where to begin? If you think about your world as a series of concentric circles, you'll discover a wealth of opportunities for building relationships. Start with your neighborhood and your children's schools. Your church probably offers a number of programs through which you can connect with others, particularly with the needy and disadvantaged. Workplace relationships are another good place to look—they form a natural bridge to building trust and growing closer to people from different backgrounds. Finally, you may want to consider getting involved with others nationally and internationally through mission trips, worthy causes, and healthy social media activities.

Putting It into Practice

Why not make your next date night a group activity? Retirement communities and nursing facilities are always grateful to have visitors. If you call ahead, it should be easy to set up a time when your group can stop by. Bring along a sampling of baked goods or some simple gifts. If anyone in your group is musically inclined, take the opportunity to lead a few songs. If that's not your cup of tea, try spending the evening just talking with the residents. You'll be amazed by what an enriching experience it can be!

Questions for Discussion

1. How can we be more community-minded and invest in the lives of other couples?
2. What does the Bible mean when it says that "we are members of one another"? How is this concept relevant to our marriage?

3. What experiences have we had in marriage that might be helpful to share with someone else? What younger couples do we know who might benefit from our input?

TRAIT 5

Conflict Resolution

As iron sharpens iron, so a man sharpens the countenance of his friend.

—Proverbs 27:17, NKJV

Conflict arises in every marriage, but God uses those struggles to help individuals and couples grow and find greater joy (James 1:2). In a thriving marriage, couples try to learn how to handle conflict. Healthy couples deal with issues right away, speak respectfully even when they disagree, and show compassion in conflict. They are willing to talk about difficult topics, try to understand each other's point of view, and forgive each other after a disagreement.

These principles have huge practical implications for your marriage in at least four distinct areas: *expectations*, *respect*, *teamwork*, and *mutual understanding*.

1. Expect rough spots

Healthy marriages are based on realistic *expectations*. It seems counterintuitive, but truly thriving couples accept conflict as one of the ground rules of marriage. Why? Because no matter how similar you and your mate may be in your interests, values, and personalities, you're still two unique individuals. You come from different backgrounds and see the world through two distinct sets of eyes. If that weren't enough, you also stand on opposite sides of the most fundamental human divide—one of you is male and the other is female! If you're honest, you know that all of this is going to lead to disagreements from time to time.

The trick here is to recognize that this isn't necessarily a bad thing. Contrary to a lot of popular wisdom, it *doesn't* mean that you and your spouse are mismatched or that your marriage is destined to fail. God wants to use this bumping and jarring to refine your relationship and cause you to grow. It's possible, then, to view conflict as a sign of life and hope. Remember, some of the greatest saints in the Bible had differences of opinion. Paul thought Mark was a slacker, and he and Barnabas had a serious falling out over whether to take Mark along on their second missionary journey (Acts 16:36–41). But years later, Paul closed his second letter to Timothy with this surprising request: "Get Mark and bring him with you [when you come to visit], because he is helpful to me in my ministry" (2 Tim. 4:11, NIV). Apparently their differences had been resolved—as can yours.

2. Fight fair

"Fighting fair" is all about maintaining *respect*. It's a matter of cultivating honesty while learning what it means to stay in love in the midst of conflict. It's a question of valuing one another enough to settle differences through negotiation rather than guerrilla warfare.

On a deeper level, fair fighting is about keeping the main thing the main thing and learning to communicate effectively. In Ephesians 4:15, Paul urges us to "speak the truth in love," adding in verse 25, "Therefore, putting away lying, 'Let each one of you speak truth with his neighbor,' for we are members of one another" (NKJV).

Respectful husbands and wives don't call each other names, make false accusations, or dredge up irrelevant incidents from the past. Instead, they practice "heart talk," which we discussed earlier. Heart talk and fair fighting are crucial to the health of your marriage. If you don't know how to resolve conflicts through negotiation, combat will take over and ultimately ruin your relationship. If spouses argue without reconciling or consistently avoid conflict altogether, their marriage is at risk for divorce. Paul recognized this same truth when he instructed the church at Galatia, "If you keep on biting and devouring each other, watch out or you will be destroyed by each other" (Gal. 5:15, NIV).

3. Work as a team

The secret to success lies in the way you handle conflict. Thriving couples know that the way they respond to their differences is far more important than how they resolve them. To state this in broader terms, they understand that, in marriage, it's the process that counts. The journey is more important than the destination. All of this implies *teamwork*.

Healthy conflict can actually become a pathway to deeper intimacy in your marriage. That's because conflict is a perfect learning situation. When you approach problems and areas of contention as a *team*, with each partner striving to understand how the other processes conflict, a light bulb goes on at the heart of your relationship. Even when you disagree, you and your spouse can make generous allowances for one another and be quick to express grace and forgiveness.

Remember Paul's words in Ephesians 4:25: You are members of one another. When one of you hurts, *both* of you hurt. That's why it's so important to act as a unit. As members of the same team, you can keep short accounts and make every effort to deal with disagreements immediately. After that, leave them behind. "Do not let the sun go down on your anger" (Eph. 4:26, ESV).

4. No losers

Healthy husbands and wives understand that, no matter what happens, they're always on the same team. They turn conflict to their advantage by working together toward *mutual understanding*. Letting go of the idea of getting their own way, they redefine "winning" as finding and implementing a solution that both spouses can feel good about. They refuse to settle for anything less.

How does it work? Our friends at Focus on the Family's Hope Restored tell us that the goal can be achieved with the following simple steps. First, establish a no-losers policy. Say to your spouse, "I will not accept any solution unless *you* love it." Second, "heart talk" the issue through until each partner thoroughly understands the other's feelings. Third, pray about it and invite God to participate in the process. Fourth, brainstorm all possible win-win solutions. Next, pick one and try it. Finally, check back in a week or two and re-evaluate. Don't be afraid to rework the plan if necessary.

Questions for Discussion

1. How can we work together to turn conflicts, arguments, or difficult decisions into sources of new strength and understanding in our marriage?
2. What are some of the major personality differences between us? How do our maleness and femaleness affect our perspectives? How can a deeper appreciation for these differences help smooth the waters the next time we're facing a serious disagreement?
3. How can friction in our relationship give us new insights about one another? How can those insights improve our ability to communicate effectively?

TRAIT 6

Coping

I have told you all this so that you may have peace in Me. Here on earth you will have many trials and sorrows. But take heart, because I have overcome the world.

—John 16:33, NLT

Every marriage faces change, stress, and crisis. Coping well requires first of all a solid understanding that challenges of this kind are inevitable. Indeed, part of the excitement and adventure of marriage comes from facing the pressure of hostile outside forces together. Healthy couples prepare for hard times and work together to overcome difficulties. They trust God, lean on each other, and are willing to seek help when they need it.

Just as learning to resolve internal conflicts helps a couple build intimacy, external challenges can also strengthen your marriage. Although painful, working through a crisis can force you to grow as individuals, giving you the maturity to confront and resolve other problems in your relationship—perhaps some you have been "stuck" on for years.

There are four keys to coping with the struggles that you and your spouse will face.

1. Expect to be tested

"Consider it all joy, my brethren, when you encounter various trials," writes James, "knowing that the testing of your faith produces endurance" (James 1:2–3, NASB). The most successful married couples are those who understand this principle and know how to put it into practice. They assume that married life is going to have its ups and downs, its good times and bad, so they don't allow unexpected changes, stresses, and crises to throw them off balance.

John and Stasi Eldredge have expressed this same idea by pointing out that every couple lives "in a great love story, set in the midst of war." By "war" they don't mean conflict between spouses, but external forces and pressures. Like any vessel on a long voyage, the ship of marriage will almost certainly have to weather some storms.

Those storms are endlessly varied: job stress, unemployment, a child with a disability, illness, in-law problems, the death of a loved one, miscarriage, infertility, infidelity, financial failure, and so on. You can probably expand the list with some personal experiences of your own. All this is completely normal, as the Apostle Paul, unmarried though he was, knew: "Those who marry will face many troubles in this life" (1 Cor. 7:28, NIV). Couples who arm themselves with this expectation have a distinct advantage over those who don't.

2. Be prepared

Equipped with the knowledge of what's coming, thriving couples take time to prepare for the difficulties that life in a fallen world is likely to send their way. They understand that the two houses described in Jesus's parable—the house built on the sand and the house built on the rock (Matt. 7:24–27)—both endured the buffeting of the wind and the rain. The only difference between the two structures was their foundations.

Because they grasp this concept, these couples don't flinch at the prospect of trouble. They don't consider it strange when trials come upon them (1 Pet. 4:12), nor do they blame one another when misfortunes arise. Instead, they take pains to anchor their marriage to the solid rock. They do this by drawing upon the strengths they derive from all of the other traits of a thriving marriage. They establish effective communication, cherish and nourish one another, build physical, emotional, and spiritual intimacy, and spend lots of enjoyable time together. In short, they strengthen their relationship during the good times so that when the bad times come they're strong enough to stand against the storm.

3. Work as a team

A thriving marriage is a team. Husbands and wives who have healthy, vibrant relationships face adversity side by side. They anticipate domestic hardships. They work together to get on the same page when faced with stressful or critical situations. They bear one another's burdens (Gal. 6:2) and take the view that tribulations and difficulties are, among other things, springboards to growth and improvement. In short, they're prepared to embark as fellow travelers on an adventurous journey.

It's essential to keep an eye out for the opportunities that lie hidden, like the proverbial silver lining, behind every new challenge that life brings our way. Danger and opportunity usually go together.

4. Ask for help

Finally, the couples we have in mind are not too proud to seek outside help in times of trouble. They are quick to turn to the Lord in prayer in every circumstance and aren't above admitting their needs to family members, friends, pastors, spiritual mentors, or professional counselors when it's appropriate. They understand that being strong doesn't necessarily mean going it alone.

"Call upon me in the day of trouble," says the Lord; "I will deliver you, and you shall glorify me" (Ps. 50:15, ESV). Enduring couples take this promise seriously, and so they trust God to lead, guide, protect, and provide for them in the face of all kinds of difficulties. They believe that He is faithful (1 Cor. 10:13), that He cares for them (1 Pet. 5:7), and that He will not allow them to be tested beyond what they can bear (1 Cor. 10:13).

Questions for Discussion

1. Have we ever thought of our relationship as a "great love story, set in the midst of war"? How might this description of marriage apply to ours?
2. What have the challenges we have faced as a couple shown us about the ways in which tough situations can become opportunities for learning and growth? How can our challenges strengthen our relationship as a couple?
3. What are some other ways we can keep our eyes open for unexpected opportunities as we meet the day-to-day challenges of the coming week?

TRAIT 7

Spending Enjoyable Time Together

Let your fountain be blessed, and rejoice in the wife of your youth.

—Proverbs 5:18, ESV

Sustaining love requires spending enjoyable time together. Thriving couples build a strong friendship by continuing to date. They develop meaningful traditions, spend time with each other, laugh together, and look for adventure. They find hobbies they can both enjoy. Happy couples build their lives on a foundation of common values, interests, and goals, finding a good mixture of independence and togetherness.

How much time should you spend together? Answers to that question vary, but if you ask the best researchers, they generally respond "as much as you can," recommending eight to fifteen hours per week.

Naturally, the *quantity* of time husbands and wives spend together is only one piece of the puzzle. *Quality* is also crucial to the health of your relationship. There are four critical ingredients in the togetherness that enables a marriage to thrive: regularity, variety, adventure, and fun. Let's examine each of them in more detail.

1. Regularity

In marriage, opportunities to enjoy one another's company should not be few and far between. On the contrary, they have to be part of the fabric of a couple's life, and therefore a priority. Time spent together doesn't just happen.

This is why it's so important to plan regular outings and date nights, doing whatever it takes—arranging for babysitters, carving time out of busy work schedules—to make sure these engagements are faithfully kept. *Both* spouses need to follow the example of the bride in the Song of Solomon: "By night on my bed I sought the one I love; I sought him but did not find him. 'I will rise now,' I said, 'and go about the city; in the streets and in the squares I will seek the one I love'" (3:1–2, NKJV). In other words, you need to pursue one another just as you did back in the days before you were married. If you want time to share your hearts, your hopes, and your dreams with each other, you've got to fight for it.

2. Variety

Current research indicates that thriving couples draw strength, energy, and life from being in one another's company. This doesn't mean, of course, that they spend *all* their time together. Healthy, vibrant relationships require breathing space, the ebb and flow of independence and togetherness. Make room for novelty and variety, working an element of the unexpected into your date night plans.

Avoid routine. As Christ said, "Behold, I make all things new" (Rev. 21:5, KJV). Add a judicious pinch of spice now and then. It's a matter of achieving the right balance—like finding your rhythm in the dance and then improvising steps just for the fun of it. Even if it means something as simple as eating at a different restaurant or going to a different movie theater every week, it's important to keep things interesting by changing the pattern.

3. Adventure

"Come, my beloved," says the Shulamite in Solomon's Song, "let us go forth to the field; let us lodge in the villages. Let us get up early to the vineyards; let us see if the vine has budded, whether the grape blossoms are open, and the pomegranates are in bloom. There I will give you my love" (Song of Sol. 7:11–12, NKJV).

Variety introduces a touch of adventure and excitement to a couple's time together. An outing doesn't have to be big, dramatic, risky, or outlandish in order to be adventurous. It simply has to include an element of the new, the unusual, or the unexpected. The idea is to keep yourselves just a little bit off balance so that you can benefit from the enriching experience of reacting to new things together.

4. Fun

Finally, when date nights are adventurous and exciting, even in understated ways, they're also fun. This is essential. Research shows that new activities activate the brain's reward system, producing excitement, exhilaration, and joy. Husbands and wives who have fun together strengthen the bonds that unite them without even realizing what they're doing. In a hundred different ways, they give themselves powerful incentives to stick together and keep coming back for more.

Happy couples find ways to keep this kind of hilarity and fun alive in their relationship, developing meaningful traditions and rituals characterized by laughter and playfulness. They don't just live under the same roof and sleep in the same bed. What's more, they keep their relationship vibrant by allowing it to breathe—and by celebrating the surprising and serendipitous side of life every chance they get.

Putting It into Practice

Here's an idea that may help you make your next date night a real adventure. Try having a "progressive dinner" on the town. Start out the evening by stopping at a place that's known for its appetizers. After that, move on to the finest salad bar in the area. Want soup? Find some out-of-the-way café that specializes in creative recipes and give one of them a try. From there you can go straight to the main course by visiting an establishment famous for its gourmet entrées. For dessert, choose your favorite ice cream shop, a specialty bakery, or some other restaurant that serves up elegant sweets. If you can manage all this on foot, so much the better. If you have to take the car, make the most of your drive time by choosing the scenic route.

Questions for Discussion

1. How can we spend time together in new, exciting, and unexpected ways?
2. How can we, together, become more intentional and aggressive about clearing our calendars to make more time for one another?
3. If we had to come up with an idea for a really fun and adventurous outing, what would it be? What would we like to do that we've never done together before?

TRAIT 8

Healthy Individuals

I have counsel and sound wisdom;
I have insight; I have strength.

—Proverbs 8:14, ESV

A marriage is only as strong as the two people in it, and a healthy marriage is made up of two healthy individuals. Thriving couples focus on how each can be a better spouse (Eph. 4:15) while continuing to grow spiritually, emotionally, physically, and mentally as individuals. A healthy marriage makes room for self-care and self-improvement. The partners know that they can't be everything to each other. As a result, each learns to rely on God to meet his or her deepest needs.

It would be fair to say that a solid understanding of this basic truth is more desperately needed in our time than ever before. Today's culture has many married people so confused that they are running in relationship circles. Some have been so wounded that they find it difficult to see their true potential. Others have simply lost sight of what they were born to do—what they were *created* to do—so that they no longer understand their purpose. Without this realization, they can't hope to have the thriving marriage God has planned for them.

It's common sense that healthy individuals make for healthy relationships. Here are some ideas about how you and your spouse can achieve the happy and lasting relationship you want.

1. Individuality

Many people come to the marital relationship with flawed expectations. They assume that marriage is designed to cure their personal ailments, that their spouse will make them whole. They don't realize that they've got the whole thing backward.

Marriage is the mysterious one-flesh union of two distinct lives and personalities (Gen. 2:24). This union is a blending, not a cloning. It's a partnership in which sharply defined differences—not merely the difference between male and female, but the distinctions between two separate individuals—come together and complement one another. These differences should be affirmed and enhanced. If you downplay them, suppress them, or attempt to erase them, you have nothing to offer to your mate. Remember, God has created each of us uniquely in His image (Gen. 1:27) so that we may become ourselves and then blend with another.

Mystery is absolutely essential to romance. Boredom can be the death knell in any relationship. Many couples find themselves "falling out of love" when they become convinced that they've learned everything there is to know about one another. That's one reason it's so important for spouses to work on preserving and celebrating their separate identities as two distinct persons.

2. Self-care

If you've done much flying, you can probably recite the following from memory:

> In the event of a change in cabin pressure, an oxygen mask will automatically appear in front of you. To start the flow of oxygen, pull the mask toward you. Place it firmly over your nose and mouth, secure the elastic band behind your head, and breathe normally. Although the bag does not inflate, oxygen is flowing to the mask. If you are traveling

> with a child or someone who requires assistance, secure your own mask first, and then assist the other person.

This brief announcement communicates a principle that is basic to all healthy relationships: you have to secure your own "oxygen mask" before you can help others. Spouses need to take time for self-nurture—time to be alone with the Lord, to be with friends (he with his and she with hers), to develop personal interests, and to engage in lifelong learning. As Gary Smalley explains, good self-care sets you up for relationship success: "If you don't take care of yourself, you have no overflow."

Marriage is about giving, but you can't give your spouse what you don't have. If you're fatigued, depressed, or saddled with a sense of guilt or inferiority, you're in no position to encourage or build up your partner. Before you can love him or her, you have to love yourself (Lev. 19:18; Matt. 22:39). This is where the give and take of a healthy marital relationship really begins.

3. The marriage triangle

As believers, we take it for granted that the most important aspect of self-care and self-improvement is spiritual in nature. If a thriving marriage is a Christ-centered marriage, it follows that a thriving marriage will be made up of two Christ-centered individuals.

Marriage is like a triangle with God at the apex. As husband and wife rise toward the goal of becoming more like Christ, they also grow closer to one another. In the process, the bond that unites them becomes stronger.

The implication is clear: If you want to love your spouse, love God with all your heart. Make sure your life is centered in your relationship with Him. Remember the words of the psalmist: "Whom have I in heaven but you? And there is none upon earth that I desire besides you" (Ps. 73:25, NKJV). To build a marriage that will go the distance, build your hopes upon the rock-solid foundation of faith in Jesus Christ.

4. Independence and dependence

God has made each one of us with a set of needs that He alone is capable of fulfilling. To expect another human being to assume His role is to put that person under an intolerable burden. The first step to building a thriving marriage is to let the Lord give you the meaning and security only He can provide. Only then will you truly know what you have to offer in your relationship with your spouse.

A healthy marriage leaves room for relational margins and breathing space. It includes time apart as well as time together. Thriving couples understand that husbands and wives can't be *everything* to each other. Sinful, imperfect, finite people, they don't have that capacity. That's God's role. But if a man and woman are willing to cling to Him in faith and grow together in the knowledge of His grace, they can have a deeply satisfying marriage that will stand the test of time.

Questions for Discussion

1. How can I help you grow spiritually? Emotionally? Physically? Professionally? How can I encourage you and give you the freedom to pursue your own personal growth so that you can make an even greater contribution to our marriage?
2. Do you feel that there's enough "breathing space" in our relationship? If not, what can we do to solve the problem?
3. What one question have you always wanted to ask me? What can I do to help you know me better?

TRAIT 9

Nourish

Blessed is everyone who fears the Lord, who walks in his ways. When you eat the labor of your hands, you shall be happy, and it shall be well with you. Your wife shall be like a fruitful vine in the very heart of your house, your children like olive plants all around your table.

—Psalm 128:1–3, NKJV

Couples who nourish each other put love into action. They sacrifice by putting the other's needs above their own. Both members of a thriving marriage strive to discover what helps the other feel loved. They encourage each other, support each other's goals, and say through their actions, "You are valuable to me."

Cherishing is an attitude, but nourishing is an action. To cherish is to love, esteem, and treasure someone in your heart. To nourish is to communicate that love in ways the other person finds meaningful. Nourishing is all about building up, helping your spouse achieve his or her God-given potential. The key is to encode the message in a language he or she can understand.

Effective nourishing involves four steps: exercising the *will*, putting the will into *action*, supporting actions with *words*, and learning to speak your spouse's special "love language." Let's take a closer look.

1. Will

Nourishing is based on a resolution to identify your spouse's strengths and find creative ways to stimulate them, draw them out, and enhance them. This doesn't happen automatically. You must decide to do it, exercising foresight and envisioning who and what your mate can become as you feed him or her with the proper spiritual food.

The key text here is Ephesians 5:29: "No one ever hated his own flesh, but nourishes and cherishes it, just as Christ also does the church." Paul reminds the Church that people rarely neglect their own bodies and that caring for your spouse's needs should get that level of attention. It's a matter of loving your partner as you love yourself (Luke 6:31).

Bottom line: You are responsible for helping your spouse become more like Christ. You're to care about and spur his or her ongoing spiritual, mental, and emotional growth. You're not responsible for the outcome, but you are responsible for nourishing this aspect of his or her life. Most people have never looked at marriage in this light before. If you haven't, you need to make up your mind to see it this way from now on.

2. Actions

If cherishing is an attitude, nourishing is the actions that stem from that attitude. In general, they boil down to service—the selfless, other-oriented kind of service that Jesus exemplified when He washed His disciples' feet. As He explained, "Now that I, your Lord and Teacher, have washed your feet, you also should wash one another's feet. I have set you an example that you should do as I have done for you" (John 13:14–15, NIV).

The Apostle Paul reflected this same mindset when he wrote to the church at Philippi:

> Do nothing out of selfish ambition or vain conceit. Rather, in humility value others above yourselves, not looking to your own interests but each of you to the interests of the

> others. In your relationships with one another, have the same mindset as Christ Jesus: who, being in very nature God, did not consider equality with God something to be used to his own advantage; rather, He made Himself nothing by taking the very nature of a servant, being made in human likeness. (Phil. 2:3–7, NIV)

This is what selfless service is all about.

3. Words

"My little children," wrote the Apostle John, "let us not love in word or in tongue, but in deed and in truth" (1 John 3:18, NKJV). Every husband and wife needs to learn how to put this verse into practice. But it's important to add that this does *not* mean that words don't count. They do.

Indeed, words carry great power. Genesis 1:3 tells us that God called the universe into being simply by *speaking*. And as Proverbs 18:21 affirms, "Death and life are in the power of the tongue" (ESV). Like God, in whose image we are made, we have the ability to tear down or build up with our words. It's a sobering thought.

Nourishing means coming alongside your mate in moments of weakness, speaking uplifting words, and offering needed support. This is why the writer of Hebrews exhorts us to "encourage one another daily, while it is still 'today'" (Heb. 3:13, NLT). If you don't provide your spouse with this kind of daily spiritual sustenance, you're essentially starving him or her. And when that happens, the whole relationship suffers.

4. Finding your mate's love language

The marriage counselor Gary Chapman says that every individual has a primary "love language." You have to learn to speak that language if you want that person to feel loved. You can talk all you want, but unless you master the correct expression, there's a good chance your spouse won't even hear your professions of undying devotion. According to Dr. Chapman, there are five basic love languages:

1. *Words of affirmation.* Some people thrive on being verbally recognized and acknowledged. If your spouse falls into this category, realize that he or she craves your words of praise and appreciation.
2. *Acts of service.* The old saying "Actions speak louder than words" is especially true for certain persons. If your mate is one of them, you'll be amazed at what an impression you can make simply by taking out the trash.
3. *Receiving gifts.* There are others who attach a great deal of significance to receiving gifts. It doesn't have to be expensive or elaborate. Remember, it's the thought that counts.
4. *Quality time.* Still other husbands and wives value the gift of time more than anything else. Give this person your undivided attention if you really want him or her to know how much you care.
5. *Physical touch.* Finally, skin on skin contact is highly important to some persons. If physical affection is your spouse's primary love language, nothing will communicate your love more clearly than a simple touch or kiss.

Do you want to help your spouse grow and flourish? Then learn his or her love language and start to use it. You'll be surprised what a difference it will make!

Questions for Discussion

1. What are our special "love languages"? Fill in the blank: "I feel loved when you _______."
2. What are some ways we can learn to speak one another's love languages more effectively?
3. What does it mean to "wash one another's feet" in the context of *our* marriage?

TRAIT 10

Physical Intimacy

Like a lily among the thorns, so is my
darling among the maidens.
Like an apple tree among the trees of the forest,
so is my beloved among the young men.
In his shade I took great delight and sat down,
And his fruit was sweet to my taste.
He has brought me into his banquet hall,
and his banner over me is love.
Sustain me with raisin cakes, refresh me
with apples, because I am lovesick.
Let his left hand be under my head and
his right hand embrace me.

—Song of Solomon 2:2–6, NASB

Mutually satisfying physical intimacy requires the recognition that sex is God's gift to a married couple, enabling husband and wife to experience the most profound intimacy possible—*two becoming one flesh* (Gen. 2:24). Thriving couples are willing to discuss what they like and dislike sexually and make adjustments to meet each other's needs. Their intimacy is marked by affection and warmth, and they understand that developing a healthy sexual relationship is a lifelong process that requires adaptability and communication.

In a strong, healthy marriage, the partners don't regard sex as a chore or obligation. Instead, they see it as a delightful dance in which each spouse puts the other's needs and interests first and explores ways of giving sexually to his or her "other half."

Here are a few of the most important steps in this marvelous dance:

1. Laying the foundation

We begin with the assumption that sex and sexuality really do matter, that they are fundamental to the marital relationship. God Himself cares deeply about this aspect of the relationship between husband and wife. Rooted not only in the Creator's original design for the human race but in man's identity as the image of God, sexuality is rooted in the Divine Nature itself: "So God created man in His own image; in the image of God He created him; male and female He created them" (Gen. 1:27, NKJV). Sexual union is essential to becoming "one flesh" (Gen. 2:24). A high regard for the "marriage bed" (Heb. 13:4)—the biblical image of Israel's relationship with Yahweh and Christ's relationship with the Church—is central to the Christian faith, as the Song of Solomon, Hosea, the sixteenth chapter of Ezekiel, Ephesians 5:22–33, and Revelation 21:2 powerfully illustrate.

2. Priming the pump

In a number of subtle and not-so-subtle ways, our culture tries to persuade us that sex is most potent when most isolated from the rest of our day-to-day experience. The most exciting encounters, we are led to believe, are those that take place outside the circle of the familiar and the mundane. Intimacy with your "old lady" or "old man" is assumed to be about as thrilling as a bowl of cold oatmeal. But Scripture adopts an entirely different point of view: sex is all about knowledge—the Hebrew word is *yada'*—of the other person, a thorough, exhaustive knowledge that embraces complete mutuality and total sharing in every area of life.

All this suggests that you have to prime the pump of passion by keeping full-fledged *romance* alive at the center of your relationship. You can do this through date nights, candlelit dinners, and generous amounts of heart-to-heart conversation. This is a truth that our X-rated society rarely acknowledges: truly enjoyable and meaningful sex derives its heat not from wanton sensuality but from the gentle, human touch of tender, romantic love.

3. "In-othering"

"You shall love your neighbor"—and that includes your husband or wife—"as yourself" (Matt. 22:39, ESV). Herein lies the real secret behind romantic love between the sexes and the physical bond in which it finds consummation. Charles Williams, a member of C. S. Lewis's legendary literary circle the Inklings, called it the mystery of "in-othering" or "co-inherence." It's the marvel of "me in you" and "you in me." Williams's term encapsulates perfectly how a love affair grows into a genuine marriage and how a genuine marriage is transformed into a way of the soul—a gateway to deeper knowledge and experience of God Himself. "For we are members of His body," writes the Apostle Paul, "of His flesh and of His bones" (Eph. 5:30, NKJV).

No wonder research indicates that a foundation of true spiritual intimacy and a shared faith in God is one of the most important predictors of the success and longevity of a marriage. Couples with such a foundation know what marital sex is *for* and what it *means.* They see their own union in the light of that greater Union toward which all things are moving.

4. Keeping it in context

Deeply meaningful sex is like a wedding cake: you build it layer by layer. You start at the most basic level and work your way up. You initiate a connection in some small and simple way and then maintain it and elaborate on it as you move forward. The act of intercourse could be compared to the icing on the cake. It's the finishing touch you put on a painting that you've labored long and painstakingly to get "just right."

This is what Dr. Kevin Leman had in mind when he chose the title *Sex Begins in the Kitchen* for his bestselling book on marital intimacy. Rather than conjuring up lurid images of passionate embraces underneath the dining room table, he hoped to convey the idea that sex is actually an expression of the care a couple shows for one another in all areas of life—in communicating, in sharing thoughts and feelings, and even in helping out around the house. What happens in the bedroom may actually be the final link in a chain of events that began hours earlier when your fingers touched while washing the dishes together.

Questions for Discussion

For your next date night, watch a romantic comedy together and think about the parallels between the typical "guy gets girl" plot and the biblical story of God's pursuit of mankind—the greatest romance of all time. Prepare by reading the Song of Solomon or the book of Hosea.

1. How has this date enabled us to put the concept of marital intimacy into the bigger picture of married life as a whole? What does it mean to *know* one

another on every level of human experience and interaction? How does physical intimacy put a bow on this package?

2. What are some ways we can get to know each other better, build intimacy, and engage in simple affectionate contact throughout the coming week?

TRAIT 11

Shared Responsibility

Bear one another's burdens, and so fulfill the law of Christ.

—Galatians 6:2, ESV

Sharing responsibility means being on the same team. Thriving couples recognize their unique God-given roles and abilities and work together to manage everyday responsibilities. Employing their individual gifts and talents, they divide household chores fairly (Phil. 2:4). They work to reach a consensus so that both partners feel satisfied with the distribution of responsibility.

In the opening chapter of Genesis, we're told that the first thing God did after creating Adam and Eve "in His image, male and female," was to entrust them with a shared responsibility: "Be fruitful and multiply; fill the earth and subdue it; have dominion over the fish of the sea, over the birds of the air, and over every living thing that moves on the earth" (Gen. 1:28, NKJV). Cooperation was basic to the divine design for marriage from the very beginning.

By contrast, if you feel you are in a never-ending battle over household responsibilities and roles, your relationship begins to feel adversarial. If you and your spouse go from being teammates to opponents, your marriage will quickly start to feel unsafe. And when unresolved power struggles lead to a relational tug-of-war over who will do what in the home, the result can fracture the bond that holds a couple together.

How do you avoid that kind of disaster? Here are a few ideas:

1. Define the problem

Once upon a time men and women entered into matrimony with very clear ideas about how the division of labor would be handled: *he* would go off to work and "bring home the bacon"; *she* would stay home, cook, clean, and raise the children. Things are different now. Today many husbands and wives perceive the allotment of housework as unfair and end up in conflict.

The problem is complicated because even in twenty-first-century America it's still common to think in terms of "male" and "female" chores, even though the Bible doesn't specifically support the notion that only women should cook and only men should calculate the budget and finances. Whether they realize it or not, couples tend to take their cues from their parents' example. This can lead to problems if unspoken assumptions and misunderstandings are allowed to explode in anger and arguments over the sharing of household tasks. Recognizing and exposing the sources of this conflict is the first step toward a solution.

The good news is that according to a Pew Research poll, sharing household chores ranks as the third-highest issue associated with a successful marriage—behind only faithfulness and good sex. This means that if you can learn to share chores, your marriage will have one of the hallmarks of unity.

2. "Into me, see"

Have you heard about the *other* way of writing the word "intimacy"—"INTO ME, SEE"? There's valuable marital wisdom in this clever play on words.

For modern married couples, a fair and mutually satisfactory plan for dividing up household chores begins with mutual understanding. It's a matter of really knowing your mate inside and out, learning about his or her special gifts and talents, finding out what makes him or her tick, and discovering what he or she really enjoys doing.

I've already mentioned Charles Williams's idea of "co-inherence." As he saw it, true intimacy is not so much a matter of *seeing into* one's mate as it is of *being in* one's mate. It's about two becoming one flesh—of identifying so closely with another person that the two of you start finishing each other's sentences and looking at the world from one another's point of view.

When it's "I in you and you in me," nobody has to ask any questions. There's no need to jockey for position or fight for a fair division of labor. The further a man and a woman move into the core of that mysterious phenomenon called co-inherence, the less they have to haggle over who cooks dinner and who takes out the trash. And it's at that point that the marriage really begins to work. It's all a matter of getting your priorities straight.

3. Lay it on the table

By this point it should be obvious that this is another one of those areas in marriage where good communication is absolutely essential. If you want to get a handle on your respective expectations for the relationship and gain a deeper appreciation for your spouse's unique abilities and talents, you need to talk about these things openly and honestly. If you can be flexible enough to allow for exceptions to accepted "rules" and work out a division of labor that places more emphasis upon each spouse's gifts than on his or her sex, you'll discover that it is possible to negotiate a plan that's agreeable to both partners.

Remember, the way a person is "wired" or designed by God can contribute to widely different expectations within a household. Some spouses do more housework because they actually prefer tidier homes. Others enjoy a house with that "lived-in" look. If you want to work together as a team, you have to begin by discussing these differences and achieving a meeting of the minds.

4. Make your own rules

Couples with vibrant and successful relationships tend to be those who have found mutually satisfactory ways of settling the "chore wars" between themselves. In other words, these husbands and wives pay relatively little attention to the shifting norms of contemporary society or the expectations of family and friends. Instead, they make it their goal to function as a unit. They understand that the only thing that matters is how they work together, not what other people think. Through discussion, negotiation, and written agreements they hammer out a plan that defines roles and divides household responsibilities fairly.

Once you reach this stage in the game, it's important to write everything down and make a chart that clearly designates each portion of the overall workload as "yours," "mine," or "ours." This agreement should be revisited and updated from time to time to accommodate the changing seasons of life. The secret here is to redefine "winning" as something that makes *both* spouses happy.

Questions for Discussion

1. What does it mean for husband and wife to become "one"? How can we move in that direction without denying our differences and giving up our unique personalities?

2. Do our roles and responsibilities play to our individual strengths in marriage? How would a deeper sense of oneness affect the way we think about household chores and our division of labor?
3. What are some other ways we can "see into" each other and develop greater marital unity?

TRAIT 12

Spiritual Intimacy

"For this reason a man shall leave his father and mother and be joined to his wife, and the two shall become one flesh." This is a great mystery, but I speak concerning Christ and the church.

—Ephesians 5:31–32, NKJV

Spiritual intimacy is all about having a strong commitment to Christ as the centerpiece of marriage (Eph. 2:20). Together and individually, husband and wife pursue a deep relationship with Christ. With a shared faith and worldview, a couple can tackle challenges and seek God's guidance together. In a thriving marriage, couples participate in spiritual practices together, seeking to become more like Christ, individually and as a couple.

To say this another way, the couples who have the best chance of going the distance in marriage are those who regard Jesus as Lord of their relationship and the unseen Ruler and Master of their home.

Why should this be so? And what can you do to shore up the spiritual foundations of your marriage? Answers to these questions fall into the following four categories:

1. The miracle of marriage

Male and female. Two in one. This, according to Scripture, is what marriage is all about. The union represented here may be one of the greatest miracles in all of creation. But it's also something more. For in addition to everything else marriage means for a man and a woman, it has a deep spiritual significance—an eternal and cosmic significance, if you will. At the highest level, it is an unparalleled working image of the seeking and saving Love of our Creator and Savior—the Love that compels Him to unite Himself to His people in a mystical bond of eternal fellowship and never-ending interpersonal give and take.

This is why the Apostle Paul says that the mystery of marriage is, at its core, a picture of the relationship between Christ and His Church (Eph. 5:32). As we've seen elsewhere, the writers of Scripture from Genesis to Revelation consistently turn to the husband-wife relationship when they want to help us understand the dealings of God with man. Couples who grasp this idea and really believe it are able to approach their marriages from an entirely new perspective, seeing their relationship as a total partnership—a one-flesh union within which spouses cultivate intimacy and interpersonal communication at every level.

This does *not* mean that "secular" or "spiritually mixed" marriages are second-rate in any way. Marriage is God's gift to *all* mankind. A Buddhist or Muslim marriage is as valid as a marriage between two Christians. Nevertheless, we are convinced that it is only "in Christ" that marriage can reach its full potential. What's more, we would suggest that in a purely practical sense, marriages lacking this shared spiritual foundation are at a serious disadvantage. The absence of a common faith represents a serious gap in any couple's relationship.

2. Spiritual discipline

Just as it can be a struggle to build physical, emotional, and relational intimacy in your marriage, many couples discover that it's difficult to be *spiritually* intimate with one another. The reasons for this are similar to the reasons why it's difficult to build intimacy in other areas: limited time, a busy life, and the demands of children, career, and, yes, even church. It's hard enough to find a few minutes for personal prayer and Bible reading, let alone time for prayer or Scripture study with your spouse!

Just as romance with your beloved requires discipline and attention, spiritual growth, both individually and in your marriage, doesn't happen automatically. Paul had this truth in mind when he urged Timothy, "Be diligent to present yourself approved to God, a worker who does not need to be ashamed, rightly dividing the word of truth" (2 Tim. 2:15, NKJV), and when he told the Thessalonians, "Pray without ceasing" (1 Thess. 5:17, NKJV).

It may sound daunting, but it's simply a question of inviting God into your everyday routine. As Brother Lawrence put it in *The Practice of the Presence of God*, "Our sanctification depends not on changing our works, but in doing for Jesus' sake that which commonly we do for our own."

3. Diversity in unity

Marriage is more than two people getting along under the same roof. It's a reflection of the Love that guides and directs the motion of the entire universe—the Love of Christ, who came to "serve and give His life a ransom for many" (Mark 10:45). Couples who share this understanding stand the best chance of experiencing the joys of marriage at their fullest.

This doesn't mean, of course, that your spiritual journey has to be exactly the same as your spouse's. Nor does it imply that the two of you will always prefer the same styles of worship or derive the same degree of benefit from different types of study or different forms of prayer. God has given to each person a unique spiritual temperament, and we can't hope to serve Him with integrity if we don't remain true to ourselves. In a healthy marriage spouses are free to affirm these differences and to learn from one another as they grow together toward the common goal of becoming more like Jesus. It's a matter of learning to become one in Christ alone; "For He Himself is our peace, who has made both one, and has broken down the middle wall of separation" (Eph. 2:14, NKJV).

4. "Christian" vs. "Christ-centered"

This leads to one last thought. When we're talking about spiritual intimacy, it's crucial to distinguish between a marriage that simply involves two Christians and a genuinely *Christ-centered* marriage, in which both partners acknowledge the presence and the authority of Christ, who makes an observable difference in their lives. It's a three-cornered relationship that places God at the apex of the triangle. If husband and wife don't share their faith by praying together, studying Scripture together, worshiping together, and reaching out together to others in Jesus' name, there can be no real intersection of their lives at the deepest level of the heart. Therefore, "Whatever you do in word or deed, do all in the name of the Lord Jesus, giving thanks to God the Father through Him" (Col. 3:17, NKJV).

Questions for Discussion

1. What are some practical steps we can take to cultivate spiritual intimacy at the heart of our marriage?
2. Who has been most influential in shaping our view of God?
3. What have we been learning in our personal prayer and Scripture reading? What sermons have especially affected us?
4. How can we pray for one another?

EPILOGUE

The Future of Marriage

With marriage now redefined, we can expect to see the marginalization of those with traditional views and the erosion of religious liberty. The law and culture will seek to eradicate such views through economic, social, and legal pressure. With marriage redefined, believing what virtually every human society once believed about marriage will increasingly be deemed a malicious prejudice to be driven to the margins of culture.

—Ryan Anderson

As I've chronicled in this book and elsewhere, marriage has been the target of many deeply concerning attacks over the past few decades. The marriage rate continues to plummet. The rates of cohabitation and out-of-wedlock birth are still climbing. Although the divorce rate has remained level since the mid-1980s, it's still dangerously high.

Yet despite the troubling trends, I don't believe the twilight of marriage is upon us. That's because marriage is a natural institution that no society can live without. This is true for all cultures throughout the world, past and present, primitive or developed. Secular anthropologists recognize this. In fact, Edward Westermarck wrote in his landmark *History of Human Marriage* (1891), "As for the origin of the institution of marriage, I consider it probable that it has developed out of primeval habit."

Trying to do away with marriage, a natural institution and the first one that God established, is like pushing a volleyball underwater and expecting it to stay there. Our cultural elites can try to keep marriage down, but human nature gives it certain buoyancy.

This is exactly what happened with Christianity in the early decades of the twentieth century. The rise of science and "reason" (as if religion were irrational!) was supposed to have put an end to religious "superstition." Many elites believed that by the time we reached the third millennium, religion would be extinct. It hasn't happened, and it's not going to happen. As a matter of fact, biblical Christianity is stronger than it has been in the past few hundred years, particularly in developing countries.

LOOKING AHEAD

In a curious way, we are actually seeing something of a revival of marriage among young adults. Each generation reacts to the generation that came before it. Those who grew up during the Great Depression went on to become one of the most prosperous generations in American history. Having seen their parents struggle, they were determined to build a different kind of life. The next generation, taking for granted the financial security that their parents' quiet, faithful, hardworking lives produced, heeded Timothy Leary's call to "turn on, tune in, and drop out." As they grew into adulthood, they became the most divorced generation in history, their own children growing up as latch-key kids, many of them bouncing back and forth between homes.

This is where a mild marriage renaissance seems to be happening. Today's young people don't want to be the free-love, anti-marriage generation. Ask them. We hear of the hook-up culture today, but when asked, young people say they don't want it. They just don't know what else to do. Our Boundless ministry to young single adults at Focus on the Family tells me young people don't even know how to date anymore. But they want to. They *want* marriage and family. In fact, for many it's their top life goal. The data have shown this time and time again. Marriage, like a volleyball in water, is naturally rising back to the surface.

Yet this generation remains leery about committing to marriage, because they've seen their parents meander miserably through their own marital relationships. Having lost the script for family life, they are convinced they can't succeed at marriage. Paralyzed by fear, they settle for cohabitation, either as a placeholder—a "good enough for now" relationship—or as a road test for a relationship that seems to have promise. Only 25 percent of cohabiters today say they have no interest in marrying one day. The remaining 75 percent would like to marry at some point. Unfortunately, as we know, there's scarcely anything more damaging to a couple's chances for marital success than living together before marriage.

SIZING UP THE CHALLENGE

The Christian Church and organizations like Focus on the Family are facing difficult times but also tremendous opportunities. Think about it. This generation, the largest this nation has ever seen, wants what we have to offer. They desperately want a settled life that has meaning, security, and stability. We need to affirm that desire and convince them it is achievable.

More resources for building and maintaining a thriving and successful marriage—books, experiential programs, courses, radio shows, and so on—are available to today's young adults than any generation in history has enjoyed. They need to know that churches are marriage-building and lifesaving stations, repositories of practical wisdom and encouragement.

In conclusion, I want to address the Christian community. It is our responsibility to show the world God's purpose for marriage. We can't lay it at the feet of others. Yes, we must push for laws that respect the truth about marriage, but we need to show others the way forward. This is our moment. It's time to take responsibility for our own marriages and to help those around us with their marital unions.

I often tell fellow believers in Christ that God is in control and I trust Him. As an orphaned child, I trusted Him in a childlike way. I still do. He is grieved but never shocked. I believe we find ourselves in this difficult season because the Lord allows us, for both good and bad, the desires of our hearts. If we His people begin to live according to His Word, our divorce rates will decrease even as the world's increase.

What if, as in ancient Rome, citizens looked with intrigue, wonder, and amazement at the behavior and practices of Christians? What if the world saw among believers thriving marriages; warm, healthy relationships; and happy homes? Would they not say, "We need what they have"? I believe they would. It would change the trajectory of the cultural debate. It would change the lives of millions of people, including the innocent children currently caught up in rising dysfunction.

This is our challenge and God's command.

May we Christians be worthy of Him "who began a good work in you" and in due time "bring it to completion at the day of Jesus Christ" (Phil. 1:6, ESV).

Acknowledgments

None of my writing projects takes place in isolation, rather they represent a collaborative effort of many gifted and talented individuals. Chief among them is my colleague, friend, and writing partner Paul Batura. His knack for capturing my heart and voice was indispensable, along with his tireless research and storytelling. I am grateful for his work in helping me craft this book. I also want to thank my dear friend and brother in Christ, Bob DeMoss, who first envisioned this project and helped bring it to fruition. Many of my Focus colleagues also contributed to the effort, including Ron Reno, Don Morgan, Dr. Greg Smalley, Tim Goeglein, Joel Vaughan, Shelly Smith, and Jim Ware. What a privilege to labor alongside so many wise and Godly men and women. I am also indebted to the great team at Regnery, including Marji Ross and Harry Crocker.

Foremost, however, is my dear wife, Jean, who is deserving of tremendous credit. I am only qualified to write about marriage because she agreed to marry me on a wing and a prayer. Her insight, wisdom, and love helped influence and shape every page in this book. I thank God for her life (Phil. 3:1).

Notes

Prologue: Why Should We Care about Marriage?

1. John C. Eastman, "Just the Facts, Ma'am: Rebutting the False 'Inevitability' Narrative," Public Discourse, April 20, 2015, http://www.thepublicdiscourse.com/2015/04/14865/.
2. Obergefell v. Hodges, 576 U.S. (2015), http://www.supremecourt.gov/opinions/14pdf/14-556_3204.pdf.
3. Ryan T. Anderson, "Supreme Court Debates Meaning of Marriage and Consequences of Judicial Redefinition," Public Discourse, April 30, 2015, http://www.thepublicdiscourse.com/2015/04/14932/.
4. Obergefell v. Hodges.
5. Jonathan V. Last, "America's Baby Bust," *Wall Street Journal*, February 12, 2013, http://www.wsj.com/articles/SB1000142412788732337520457827005 3387770718.

6. Nicole Martin, "Practice of 'Living Together' without Marriage Has Long, Complex History," Gender News, Clayman Institute for Gender Research, Stanford University, August 15, 2013, http://gender.stanford.edu/news/2013/practice-living-together-without-marriage-has-long-complex-history.
7. W. Bradford Wilcox, "The Evolution of Divorce," *National Affairs* 1, no. 1 (Fall 2009): http://www.nationalaffairs.com/publications/detail/the-evolution-of-divorce.
8. Ibid.
9. Pam Belluck, "Massachusetts Arrives at Moment for Same-Sex Marriage," *New York Times*, May 17, 2004.

Chapter One: Miracle, Mystery, and Wonder

1. G. K. Chesterton, *The Catholic Church and Conversion*, in vol. 3 of *The Collected Works of G. K. Chesterton* (San Francisco: Ignatius Press, 1990), 94.
2. C. S. Lewis, *The Four Loves* (New York: Harcourt Brace, 1960), 89.
3. Albert Mohler, "Looking Back at 'The Mystery of Marriage,'—Part One," AlbertMohler.com, August 19, 2004, http://www.albertmohler.com/2004/08/19/looking-back-at-the-mystery-of-marriage-part-one/.
4. Jim Daly, *Finding Home: An Imperfect Path to Faith and Family* (Colorado Springs: David C. Cook, 2007).
5. Michael Burlingame, *The Inner World of Abraham Lincoln* (Urbana: University of Illinois Press, 1994), 278.
6. Letter from Lincoln to Samuel S. Marshall, November 11, 1842, available online at http://publications.newberry.org/lincoln/exhibits/show/alwayshatedslavery/lincolnthewhig/profoundwonder.
7. Yasmine Hafiz, "Candace Cameron Bure Explains Being 'Submissive' to Husband," Huffington Post, January 25, 2014, http://www.huffingtonpost.com/2014/01/06/candance-cameron-bure-submissive_n_4550818.html.
8. Timothy J. Keller, *The Meaning of Marriage: Facing the Complexities of Commitment with the Wisdom of God* (New York: Dutton, 2011).
9. Quoted in John Piper and Wayne Grudem, *Recovering Biblical Manhood and Womanhood: A Response to Evangelical Feminism* (Wheaton, IL: Crossway Books, 1991).
10. John Piper, "The Mystery of Marriage," from *Desiring God*, Solid Joys, http://solidjoys.desiringgod.org/en/devotionals/the-mystery-of-marriage.

Chapter Two: From Safety Seeker to Soul Mate

1. C. S. Lewis, *Selected Literary Essays* (London: Cambridge U.P., 1969), 117.
2. Elizabeth Gilbert, *Eat, Pray, Love: One Woman's Search for Everything across Italy, India, and Indonesia* (New York: Viking, 2006).
3. Gilbert, *Committed: A Skeptic Makes Peace with Marriage* (New York: Viking, 2010).
4. Ibid.
5. Gilbert, "Confessions of a Seduction Addict," *New York Times Magazine*, June 24, 2015, http://www.nytimes.com/2015/06/28/magazine/confessions-of-a-seduction-addict.html?_r=0.
6. Aaron Ben-Zeev, "Is Serial Monogamy Worth Pursuing?," *Psychology Today*, October 31, 2008.
7. Gilbert, *Committed.*
8. See "Why Marriage Matters: Facts and Figures," For Your Marriage, http://www.foryourmarriage.org/factsfigures/.
9. W. Bradford Wilcox, "Don't Hold a Funeral for Marriage Yet," Federalist, May 19, 2015.
10. *New Castle (PA) News*, June 4, 1924.
11. Martha Garrison and Elizabeth S. Scott, *Marriage at the Crossroads* (New York: Cambridge University Press, 2012).
12. Paul R. Amato, Alan Booth, David R. Johnson, and Stacy J. Rogers, *Alone Together: How Marriage in America Is Changing* (Cambridge, MA: Harvard University Press, 2007), 12.
13. Patrick Fagan and Robert Rector, "The Effects of Divorce on America," *Backgrounder* no. 1373, Heritage Foundation, June 5, 2000, http://www.heritage.org/research/reports/2000/06/the-effects-of-divorce-on-america.
14. Pat Conroy, "Anatomy of a Divorce," *Atlantic*, November 1, 1978.
15. Edward Westermarck, *The History of Human Marriage*, vol. 1 (New York: Allerton Book Company, 1922), 26–27, 46.
16. Gary Thomas, *Sacred Marriage: What If God Designed Marriage to Make Us Holy More Than to Make Us Happy?* (Grand Rapids, MI: Zondervan, 2000).
17. George Hughes Hepworth, *The Hepworth Yearbook* (New York: E. P. Dutton, 1897).
18. Samuel Taylor Coleridge, "Letter to a Young Lady," 1822.
19. Faye Hall, *My Gift to You* (Seminole, FL: Red Sage Publishing, 2012).
20. *Plato's Symposium*, trans. Seth Benardete (Chicago: University of Chicago Press, 2001).
21. Thomas, *Sacred Marriage.*

22. Ibid.
23. Timothy Keller, "You Never Marry the Right Person," *Relevant*, January 5, 2012, http://www.relevantmagazine.com/life/relationship/features/27749-you-never-marry-the-right-person.
24. Rick Warren, "Christ-Likeness Is Produced through the Holy Spirit," Daily Hope with Rick Warren, May 21, 2014, http://rickwarren.org/devotional/english/christ-likeness-is-produced-through-the-holy-spirit.

Chapter Three: Why Marry at All?

1. Timothy J. Keller, *The Meaning of Marriage: Facing the Complexities of Commitment with the Wisdom of God* (New York: Dutton, 2011).
2. "Grandmother Is 'Most Married Woman' after Tying the Knot 23 Times," *Telegraph*, February 24, 2009, http://www.telegraph.co.uk/news/newstopics/howaboutthat/4796811/Grandmother-is-most-married-woman-after-tying-the-knot-23-times.html.
3. Ibid.
4. Jon Hilkevitch, "Looking for Mrs. Right," *Chicago Tribune*, July 12, 1990, http://articles.chicagotribune.com/1990-07-12/news/9002260830_1_glynn-scotty-wolfe-daisy-hubble-space-telescope.
5. Ibid.
6. W. Speers, "Joan Collins Files for Fourth Divorce," *Philadelphia Inquirer*, December 9, 1986.
7. Alex Heigl, "The Many Wives of Mickey Rooney," *People*, April 7, 2014.
8. Larry King, *My Remarkable Journey* (New York: Hachette Book Group, 2009).
9. Ibid.
10. Lois M. Collins, "U.S. Marriage Rate Hits New Low and May Continue to Decline," *Deseret News*, May 20, 2015, http://national.deseretnews.com/article/4535/US-marriage-rate-hits-new-low-and-may-continue-to-decline.html.
11. Lauren Fox, "The Science of Cohabitation: A Step toward Marriage, Not a Rebellion," *Atlantic*, March 20, 2014.
12. Rose Kreider, "Housing and Household Economic Statistics Division Working Paper," U.S. Bureau of the Census, September 15, 2010, https://www.census.gov/population/www/socdemo/Inc-Opp-sex-2009-to-2010.pdf.
13. "National Vital Statistics Reports," Centers for Disease Control and Prevention, http://www.cdc.gov/nchs/products/nvsr.htm.

14. Molly Triffin, "So...Why Do People Get Married, Anyway?," *Cosmopolitan*, December 4, 2012, http://www.cosmopolitan.com/sex-love/advice/g2514/why-do-people-get-married/?slide=1.
15. Janice K. Kiecolt-Glaser and Tamara L. Newton, "Marriage and Health: His and Hers," *Psychological Bulletin* 127, no. 4 (2001): 472–503.
16. Lee Robins and Darrel Regier, *Psychiatric Disorders in America: The Epidemiologic Catchment Area Study* (New York: Free Press, 1991), 64, 334.
17. Steven Stack and J. Ross Eshleman, "Marital Status and Happiness: A 17-Nation Study," *Journal of Marriage and Family* 60, no. 2 (1998): 527–36.
18. MyHealthNewsDaily, "Take Heart! A Good Marriage Protects Even after a Bypass," Fox News Health, August 22, 2011, http://www.foxnews.com/health/2011/08/22/take-heart-good-marriage-protects-even-after-bypass.html.
19. Wendy Wang and Kim Parker, "Record Share of Americans Have Never Married," Pew Research Center, September 24, 2014, http://www.pewsocialtrends.org/2014/09/24/record-share-of-americans-have-never-married/.
20. Ibid.
21. "The Decline of Marriage and Rise of New Families," Pew Research Center, November 18, 2010, http://www.pewsocialtrends.org/2010/11/18/the-decline-of-marriage-and-rise-of-new-families/.
22. Richard Godbeer, *Sexual Revolution in Early America* (Baltimore: Johns Hopkins University Press, 2002).
23. Blaise Pascal, *Pensées*, trans. A. J. Krailsheimer (London: Penguin, 1995), 75.
24. David Kinnaman, *unChristian: What a New Generation Really Thinks about Christianity—and Why It Matters* (Grand Rapids, MI: Baker Books, 2007).
25. Bruce Marshall, *The World, the Flesh and Father Smith* (Boston: Houghton Mifflin, 1945), 108.
26. Kathleen O'Brien, "Marriage Fades, but Not for Lack of Couples," Christian Century, November 19, 2010, http://www.christiancentury.org/article/2010-11/marriage-fades-not-lack-couples.
27. "60% of Americans Feel Lonely Now Turn to Social Media Network Friends," iHumanMedia, February 21, 2014, http://ihumanmedia.com/2014/02/21/60-of-americans-feel-lonely-now-turn-to-social-media-network-friends/.

28. Tricia McDermott, "Ronald Reagan Remembered," CBS News, June 6, 2004, http://www.cbsnews.com/news/ronald-reagan-remembered/.

Chapter Four: Reformed and Transformed

1. Margaret Mead, *Male and Female: A Study of the Sexes in a Changing World* (New York: Morrow, 1949).
2. Richard F. Shepard, "'Duke,' an American Hero," *New York Times*, June 12, 1979.
3. Robert Lewis, *Raising a Modern-Day Knight* (Carol Stream, IL: Tyndale House, 2007).
4. Peggy Noonan, "Welcome Back, Duke," *Wall Street Journal*, October 12, 2001.
5. Albert Mohler, "Man Up or Man Down? *Newsweek* Redefines Masculinity," AlbertMohler.com, September 23, 2010, http://www.albertmohler.com/2010/09/23/man-up-or-man-down-newsweek-redefines-masculinity/.
6. Ibid.

Chapter Five: Vive la Différence!

1. George Gilder, *Men and Marriage* (Gretna, LA: Pelican Publishers, 1986).
2. See Sir Edwin Sandy's description of women at Jamestown, reproduced at "The Indispensable Role of Women at Jamestown," Historic Jamestowne, National Park Service, http://www.nps.gov/jame/learn/historyculture/the-indispensible-role-of-women-at-jamestown.htm.
3. Gail Collins, *America's Women: 400 Years of Dolls, Drudges, Helpmates, and Heroines* (New York: Morrow, 2003), 3.
4. Ibid., 4.
5. Ibid., 3.
6. Sylvia R. Frey and Marian Morton, *New World, New Roles: A Documentary History of Women in Pre-Industrial America* (New York: Greenwood Press, 1986).
7. "The Indispensable Role of Women at Jamestown."
8. Ibid.
9. John MacArthur, *Twelve Extraordinary Women: How God Shaped Women of the Bible, and What He Wants to Do with You* (Nashville: Nelson Books, 2005).

Chapter Six: Why Children Need Both a Mother and a Father

1. Daniel Patrick Moynihan, *Meet the Press*, September 19, 1993.
2. "Stats," Fatherhood Factor, http://fatherhoodfactor.com/us-fatherless-statistics/.
3. "Births: Final Data for 2010," *National Vital Statistics Reports* 61, no. 1 (2012): http://www.cdc.gov/nchs/data/nvsr/nvsr61/nvsr61_01.pdf.
4. Jenny Tyree, "30 Years of Research That Tell Us, 'A Child Deserves a Mother and a Father,'" CitizenLink, June 17, 2010, http://www.citizenlink.com/2010/06/17/30-years-of-research-that-tells-us-a-child-deserves-a-mother-and-a-father/.
5. Kyle D. Pruett, *The Nurturing Father* (New York: Warner Books, 1987), 49.
6. Ibid.
7. Glenn T. Stanton, "Why Children Need Father-Love and Mother-Love," *John Ankerberg Show*, 2004, https://www.jashow.org/articles/society-culture-politics-2/gay-lesbian-issues/same-sex-marriage/why-children-need-father-love-and-mother-love/.
8. Carol Ann Rinzler, *Why Eve Doesn't Have an Adam's Apple: A Dictionary of Sex Differences* (New York: Facts on File, 1996), 4.
9. Larry Cahill, "Equal Does Not Equal the Same: Sex Differences in the Human Brain," *Cerebrum*, March–April 2014, http://www.ncbi.nlm.nih.gov/pmc/articles/PMC4087190/.
10. Ibid.
11. Rinzler, *Why Eve Doesn't Have an Adam's Apple*, 126.
12. Ibid., 129.
13. Ibid., 108.
14. Leonard Sax, *Why Gender Matters* (New York: Doubleday, 2005), 93.
15. Ibid., 29.
16. Suzanne Frayser, *Varieties of Sexual Experience: Anthropological Perspective on Human Sexuality* (New York: Human Relations Area File Press, 1985), 86.
17. Ibid.
18. Scott Coltrane, "Father-Child Relationships and the Status of Women: A Cross-Cultural Study," *American Journal of Sociology*, 93 (1988): 1088.
19. Stanton, "Why Children Need Father-Love and Mother-Love."
20. *Summary of Study Findings: Fathering in America* (Springdale, AR: National Center for Fathering: May 2009), http://www.fathers.com/documents/research/2009_Fathering_in_America_Summary.pdf.

21. Alemayehu Bishaw, "Poverty: 2000 to 2012," *American Community Survey Brief*, September 2013, https://www.census.gov/prod/2013pubs/acsbr12-01.pdf.
22. Bruce J. Ellis et al., "Does Father Absence Place Daughters at Special Risk for Early Sexual Activity and Teenage Pregnancy?," *Child Development* 74, no. 3: 801–21, http://www.ncbi.nlm.nih.gov/pmc/articles/PMC2764264/.

Chapter Seven: In Good Times and in Bad

1. Douglas Groothuis, "Bedeviled by My Wife's Dementia," *Christianity Today*, October 26, 2015.
2. Ibid.
3. Ibid.
4. Jack Wellman, "Top 10 Billy Graham Quotes with Commentary," *Christian Crier* (blog), Patheos, August 31, 2013, http://www.patheos.com/blogs/christiancrier/2013/08/31/top-10-billy-graham-quotes-with-commentary/.
5. Staff, "Charles Stanley, Wife Divorce; Atlanta Church Affirms Pastor," Baptist Press, May 23, 2000, http://www.bpnews.net/5874.
6. Lisa Miller, "The Fight over Billy Graham's Legacy," *Newsweek*, May 15, 2011; and Timothy C. Morgan, "Tullian Tchividjian Files for Divorce," *Christianity Today*, August 22, 2015, http://www.christianitytoday.com/gleanings/2015/august/tullian-tchividjian-files-for-divorce.html.
7. "Does Divorce Help Adults Become Happier?," chapter 4 of Alan J. Hawkins and Tamara A. Fackrell, *Should I Keep Trying to Work It Out?* (Salt Lake City: 2009), http://www.divorce.usu.edu/files/uploads/lesson4.pdf.
8. Leslie L. Bachand and Sandra L. Caron, "Ties That Bind: A Qualitative Study of Happy Long-Term Marriages," *Contemporary Family Therapy* 23, no. 1 (March 2001): http://www.academia.edu/5197358/Ties_that_Bind_A_Qualitative_Study_of_Happy_Long-Term_Marriages (January 2, 2016); and Linda Waite and Maggie Gallagher, *The Case for Marriage* (New York: Doubleday, 2000), 148.
9. Robert Coombs, "Marital Status and Personal Well-Being: A Literature Review," *Family Relations* 40, no. 1 (January 1991): 97–102; and I. M. Joung et al., "Differences in Self-Reported Morbidity by Marital Status and by Living Arrangement," *International Journal of Epidemiology* 23, no. 1 (1994): 91–97.
10. Harold J. Morowitz, "Hiding in the Hammond Report," *Hospital Practice*, August 1975, p. 39.
11. James S. Goodwin, William C. Hunt, Charles R. Key, and Jonathan M. Sarmet, "The Effect of Marital Status on Stage, Treatment, and Survival of

Cancer Patients," *Journal of the American Medical Association* 258, no. 21 (1987): 3125–30.

12. Nadine F. Marks and James D. Lambert, "Marital Status Continuity and Change among Young and Midlife Adults: Longitudinal Effects on Psychological Well-Being," *Journal of Family Issues* 19, no. 6 (1998): 652–86.
13. Ibid.
14. Elizabeth Bernstein, "Divorcé's Guide to Marriage," *Wall Street Journal*, July 24, 2012, http://www.wsj.com/articles/SB10000872396390444025204577544951717564114.
15. The website for the Gottman Institute is https://www.gottman.com/.

Chapter Eight: For the Greater Good

1. "Homily of John Paul II," Perth, Australia, November 30, 1986, https://w2.vatican.va/content/john-paul-ii/en/homilies/1986/documents/hf_jp-ii_hom_19861130_perth-australia.html.
2. Leonard Bernstein, "The Ideas of John Humphrey Noyes, Perfectionist," *American Quarterly* 5, no. 2 (1953): 162.
3. Ibid.
4. Spencer Klaw, *Without Sin: The Life and Death of the Oneida Community* (New York: Allen Lane, 1993).
5. Chris Ritter, "Speaking of Sin: Augustine, Luther, and the Inward Curve," *The Gospel Matters* (blog), January 11, 2012, https://thegospelmatters.wordpress.com/2012/01/11/speaking-of-sin-luther-augustine-and-the-inward-curv/.
6. David G. Schramm, "Divorce: The Economic Consequences to the 'Village' That Raised the Child," available online at http://www.law2.byu.edu/wfpc/forum/2007/Schramm.pdf.
7. Institute for American Values et al., "Executive Summary" of "The Taxpayer Costs of Divorce and Unwed Childbearing," no date, http://www.americanvalues.org/pdfs/coff-executive_summary.pdf.
8. Lawrence Kudlow, "Marriage Emerges as Key to Economic Growth," *New York Sun*, November 14, 2014, http://www.nysun.com/national/marriage-emerges-as-a-key/88927/.
9. W. Bradford Wilcox, Robert I. Lerman, and Joseph Price, "Strong Families, Prosperous States: Do Healthy Families Affect the Wealth of States?," American Enterprise Institute and the Institute for Family Studies, October 19, 2015, https://www.aei.org/publication/strong-families-prosperous-states/.

10. Emily Badger, "The Terrible Loneliness of Growing Up Poor in Robert Putnam's America," *Wonkblog* (blog), March 6, 2015, https://www.washingtonpost.com/news/wonk/wp/2015/03/06/the-terrible-loneliness-of-growing-up-poor-in-robert-putnams-america/.
11. Robert Rector and Rachel Sheffield, "The War on Poverty after 50 Years," *Backgrounder* no. 2955, Heritage Foundation, September 15, 2014, http://www.heritage.org/research/reports/2014/09/the-war-on-poverty-after-50-years.
12. Ryan Anderson, "Marriage: What It Is, Why It Matters, and the Consequences of Redefining It," *Backgrounder* no. 2775, Heritage Foundation, March 11, 2013, http://www.heritage.org/research/reports/2013/03/marriage-what-it-is-why-it-matters-and-the-consequences-of-redefining-it.
13. Daniel P. Moynihan, "A Dahrendorf Inversion and the Twilight of the Family: The Challenge of the Conference," in Daniel P. Moynihan, Timothy M. Smeeding, and Lee Rainwater, eds., *The Future of the Family* (New York: Russell Sage Foundation, 2004), xxi.
14. Barack Obama, "Remarks at the Selma Voting Rights March Commemoration in Selma, Alabama," transcript of March 4, 2007, remarks, American Presidency Project, http://www.presidency.ucsb.edu/ws/?pid=77042.
15. "Criminal Victimization in the United States, 2007 Statistical Tables," National Crime Victimization Survey, U.S. Department of Justice, Bureau of Justice Statistics, February 2010, Table 12; and Jenny Tyree, "The Truth about Domestic Violence in Marital versus Cohabitational Relationships," CitizenLink, June 14, 2010, http://www.citizenlink.com/2010/06/14/the-truth-about-domestic-violence-in-marital-versus-cohabitational-relationships/.
16. "Criminal Victimization in the United States, 2007 Statistical Tables."
17. Michael Gordon, "The Family Environment of Sexual Abuse: A Comparison of Natal and Stepfather Abuse," *Child Abuse and Neglect*, 13, no. 1 (1989): 121–30.
18. Robert Putnam, *Our Kids: The American Dream in Crisis* (New York: Simon & Schuster, 2015).
19. Cynthia Harper and Sara McLanahan, "Father Absence and Youth Incarceration," *Journal of Research on Adolescence* 14, no. 3 (2004), 369–97.
20. Elaine Kamarck and William Galston, "Putting Children First: A Progressive Family Policy for the 1990s," white paper from the Progressive Policy Institute, September 27, 1990, pp. 14–15.

Chapter Nine: The Sanctity of Sex

1. "Is Your Marriage Normal or Nuts?" *Reader's Digest*, May 2013.
2. Ibid.
3. Bill and Pam Farrel, *Red Hot Monogamy* (Eugene, OR: Harvest House Publishers, 2006).
4. John Naish, *Put What Where? Over Two Thousand Years of Bizarre Sex Advice* (London: Harper Element, 2005).
5. Eugene Becklard and Philip M. Howard, *Becklard's Physiology: Physiological Mysteries and Revelations in Love, Courtship, and Marriage: An Infallible Guide-Book for Married and Single Persons, In Matters of the Utmost Importance to the Human Race* (Philadelphia, 1850).
6. Henry Hanchett and Alexander Laidlaw, *Sexual Health: A Plain and Practical Guide for the People on All Matters Concerning the Organs of Reproduction in Both Sexes and All Ages* (New York: C. T. Hurlburt, 1887).
7. Edward Podolsky, *Sex Today in Wedded Life* (New York: Simon Publications, 1947).
8. Elizabeth Bernstein, "What Keeps Couples Happy Long Term," *Wall Street Journal*, February 9, 2016, http://www.wsj.com/articles/what-keeps-couples-happy-long-term-1454961956?tesla=y.
9. Authentic Intimacy, https://authenticintimacy.com/; Juli Slattery and Linda Dillow, *Passion Pursuit: What Kind of Love Are You Making?* (Chicago: Moody Publishers, 2013); Slattery, *Finding the Hero in Your Husband* (Deerfield Beach, FL: Faith Communications, 2004); and Slattery, *No More Headaches: Enjoying Sex and Intimacy in Marriage* (Carol Stream, IL: Tyndale House, 2009).
10. Dillow and Slattery, *Surprised by the Healer* (Chicago: Moody Publishers, 2016).
11. John Piper, *This Momentary Marriage* (Wheaton, IL: Crossway, 2012), 135.

Chapter Ten: Remarriage and Starting Anew

1. Mitch Albom, *The Magic Strings of Frankie Presto* (New York: Harper, 2015).
2. "National Marriage and Divorce Rate Trends," Centers for Disease Control and Prevention, November 3, 2015, http://www.cdc.gov/nchs/nvss/marriage_divorce_tables.htm.
3. Michael Smalley, "How to Have a Successful Second Marriage," Smalley.cc, April 23, 2009, http://www.smalley.cc/how-to-have-a-successful-second-marriage/.

4. See SmartStepfamilies, http://www.smartstepfamilies.com/.
5. "Is Remarriage a Step in the Right Direction?," Marriage Missions International, no date, http://marriagemissions.com/is-remarriage-a-step-in-the-right-direction/.
6. Elizabeth Bernstein, "Secrets of a Second Marriage: Beat the 8-Year Itch," *Wall Street Journal*, September 20, 2011, http://www.wsj.com/articles/SB10001424053111904106704576580652976268350.
7. Michael Smalley, "Starting Over Again," Crosswalk, March 29, 2002, http://www.crosswalk.com/family/marriage/divorce-and-remarriage/starting-over-again-505914.html.
8. Les and Leslie Parrott, *Saving Your Second Marriage Before It Starts: Nine Questions to Ask Before (and After) You Remarry* (Grand Rapids, MI: Zondervan, 2001).
9. Nicholas Wapshott, "Jane Wyman, Reagan's 'Button Nose,'" *New York Sun*, September 11, 2007.
10. Ibid.
11. "Ronald Reagan and Nancy Davis," *People*, February 12, 1996, http://www.people.com/people/archive/article/0,,20102780,00.html.
12. Nancy Reagan, *I Love You, Ronnie: The Letters of Ronald Reagan to Nancy Reagan* (New York: Random House, 2000)
13. "The Love Story," Ronald Reagan Presidential Foundation and Library, no date, http://www.reaganfoundation.org/the-love-story.aspx.
14. Kiron K. Skinner, Annelise Martin, and Martin Anderson, eds., *Reagan: A Life in Letters* (New York: Free Press, 2003), 60.
15. Divorced Moms, "10 Rules for a Happy Second Marriage," Good Men Project, October 20, 2015, http://goodmenproject.com/.

Chapter Eleven: Lessons at the End of Life

1. Harriet Beecher Stowe, *Little Foxes: Or, the Insignificant Little Habits Which Mar Domestic Happiness* (London: Bell and Daldy, 1866).
2. Mark Brinkman, *On the Brink of a Dream*, "She's a Stranger in His Mind," 2010.

Chapter Twelve: More Secrets to a Great Marriage

1. Billy Graham Evangelistic Association Staff, "Notable Quotes from Billy Graham," Billy Graham Evangelistic Association, November 5, 2009, http://billygraham.org/story/notable-quotes-from-billy-graham/.

2. Susan Gregory Thomas, "The Divorce Generation," *Wall Street Journal*, July 9, 2011, http://www.wsj.com/articles/SB10001424052702303544604576430341393583056.
3. Ibid.
4. Olivia Waring, "World's Oldest Married Couple Aged 110 and 103 Celebrate Their 90th Wedding Anniversary," Metro (UK), December 11, 2015, http://metro.co.uk/2015/12/11/worlds-oldest-married-couple-aged-110-and-103-celebrate-their-90th-wedding-anniversary-5558009/.
5. Ibid.
6. Kerri MacDonald, "Lasting Love, by the Letters," *Lens* (blog), *New York Times*, February 5, 2015, http://lens.blogs.nytimes.com/2015/02/05/lasting-love-by-the-letters/.
7. Wu Yiyao, "Golden Couple Share Secret of 80-Year Marriage," *ChinaDaily*, September 11, 2010, http://www.chinadaily.com.cn/cndy/2010-09/11/content_11288525.htm.
8. Ibid.
9. Mary Bowerman, "Here's What a Couple Married for 83 Years Can Teach You about Lasting Love," *USA Today*, February 23, 2016, http://www.usatoday.com/story/news/nation-now/2016/02/11/longest-married-couple-lasting-love-83-years/80174394/.
10. Michael Walsh, "America's 'Longest-Married Couple' Celebrates 81st Wedding Anniversary," *New York Daily News*, October 17, 2014, http://www.nydailynews.com/news/national/longest-married-couple-celebrates-81st-wedding-article-1.1528689.
11. Kate Salter, "Enduring Love: The Couples Still in Love after 50 Years Together," *Telegraph*, December 5, 2014, http://www.telegraph.co.uk/women/sex/11270204/Enduring-love-the-couples-still-in-love-after-50-years-together.html.
12. Lauren Fleishman, *The Lovers* (Amsterdam: Schilt Publishing, 2015).
13. MacDonald, "Lasting Love."
14. Fleishman, *The Lovers*, 12.
15. Ibid., 14.
16. Ibid., 36.
17. Ibid., 74.
18. Jim Daly, *The Best Advice I Ever Got on Marriage: Transforming Insights from Respected Husbands and Wives* (Brentwood, TN: Worthy Publishing, 2012).
19. Ibid., v.
20. Ibid., 13.

21. Ibid., 20.
22. Ibid., 41.
23. Evangelicals and Catholics Together, "The Two Shall Become One Flesh: Reclaiming Marriage," *First Things*, March 2015, http://www.firstthings.com/article/2015/03/the-two-shall-become-one-flesh-reclaiming-marriage-2.

Your Personalized Marriage Assessment

1. Greg Smalley and Erin Smalley, *Crazy Little Thing Called Marriage: 12 Secrets of a Lifelong Romance* (Colorado Springs: Focus on the Family, 2016).

Index